RAISING
THE
VILLAGE

TRACY SMYTH   TAMMY DEWAR

RAISING
THE
VILLAGE

HOW INDIVIDUALS AND COMMUNITIES
CAN WORK TOGETHER TO GIVE OUR CHILDREN
A STRONGER START IN LIFE

FOREWORD BY DR. CLYDE HERTZMAN, MD

Published in 2009 by
BPS Books
Toronto and New York
www.bpsbooks.net
A division of
Bastian Publishing Services Ltd.

ISBN 978-1-926645-10-0

Cataloguing in Publication data available from Library and Archives Canada.

Cover design: Gnibel
Text design and typesetting: CaseyHooperDesign.com

The information in this book is true and complete to the best of our knowledge. It is offered with no guarantees on the part of the authors or BPS Books. We specifically disclaim accuracy of the community stories submitted or as told by others. Some stories have been augmented with our personal experiences. Wherever possible, the community stories do not use personal or organizational names in hopes that readers will find personal applicability; however, the advice and strategies within may not be suitable for every individual situation. The authors and publisher disclaim all liability in connection with the use of this book.

Readers should be aware that Internet Websites offered as citations and or sources for further information may have changed or disappeared between the time this book was written and when it is read.

Printed by Lightning Source, Tennessee. Lightning Source paper, as used in this book, does not come from endangered old growth forests or forests of exceptional conservation value. It is acid free, lignin free, and meets all ANSI standards for archival-quality paper. The print-on-demand process used to produce this book protects the environment by printing only the number of copies that are purchased.

*To the Alberni Valley
Make Children First Network
– our village*

CONTENTS

PART 1
BRINGING THE VILLAGE TO LIFE

PART 2
BUILDING RELATIONSHIPS

PART 3
FRAMING LEADERSHIP

PART 4
CONSTRUCTING RELEVANCE

PART 5
SUSTAINING THE VILLAGE

FOREWORD

H uman development is at the centre of the global agenda in the twenty-first century. Our planet faces challenges that can be met only by people who are tolerant, empathic, insightful, and capable of lifelong learning. Research teaches us that the roots of these human attributes are in the earliest years. Whether children will develop into effective citizens of our century depends in part on the qualities of participation, stimulation, support, and nurturance in the environments where they spend their earliest years. We as a global community, therefore, have a strong interest in what goes on in the most intimate realms of home, family, and community. While families want to do what is best for their children, in today's world they need help from society at all levels. The question we face is how to build an effective alliance between the global and the intimate without the former destroying the latter.

The best answer is likely the one contained in this book: by tying early human development to community development. The vision is one in which senior governments create the policy frameworks and funding formulae for sustainability and local communities and their leaders make the actual decisions.

The authors are pioneers in this approach. Tracy was one of the first community-based intersectoral coordinators for early child development in British Columbia. She dealt with building community capacity; supporting and coordinating effective program and policy development; and monitoring early child development outcomes in collaboration with university researchers. Tammy brought her background in early childhood education into the picture, partnering with Tracy in leading this intersectoral community initiative.

Raising the Village is based on the insights they have gained from their special vantage point. It deserves broad dissemination, not only to community developers but also to those at senior levels in society who want to know how investments in the earliest stages of human development can support, and not undermine, local communities.

CLYDE HERTZMAN, MD, MSc, FRCPC, FRSC
Director, Human Early Learning Partnership
President, Council for Early Child Development

PREFACE

This book is for people and organizations that are looking for ways to collaborate in serving children earlier and therefore their community better.

Consider it a professional resource, a how-to book, and a practical response for building and strengthening group processes behind early years community work. We believe that relationships, leadership, relevance, and strengths are the ingredients to sustainable community collaboration. In fact, this book seeks to harness members of two groups — those involved in early childhood work and those involved in community development more generally — in order to unify their concerns, expertise, and vision into "villages" that develop communities by developing young children.

The main elements involved in building these villages are covered in five parts. First we deal with how villages are defined and brought to life. Then we discuss how to build relationships and connections, how to frame leadership, and how to construct relevance to serve children better. In the final part, we examine how to sustain the energy, commitments, and objectives of "village life."

Raising the Village acknowledges the issue of child development vulnerability and aims to reveal the hidden potential to change our world of community development work by using a focus on children. It weaves together practical information, strategies, stories with emotion and insight, and community development theory into a pattern that informs and grounds the work. The academic and hands-on components, however, are not two separate pieces; rather, they are texts that blend into one message.

We hope *Raising the Village* will inspire you to make a difference in your own community while celebrating and enhancing the work already taking place. Through this book we aim to support excellent community development practice — always keeping children front and centre.

Allow each of us to make a personal and professional statement about our own commitment to early years community development.

TRACY

I have been a community builder from an early age. I grew up as a military base brat, moving to a new country or province every two or three years. I was always the new kid and often a minority. This, I think, gave me the opportunity to practice my skills in relationship building and to deepen my insight into communities in general.

I started my career in public health but was drawn to projects and initiatives that emphasized community development. In fact, I ran from situations where I was supposed to be an "expert." With a combination of luck and strategic manoeuvring, I was able to leave the field of public health nutrition and begin coordinating an innovative initiative called Make Children First. My teachers in this and subsequent work have been the mobilized force of passionate and committed service providers and volunteers who make up the heart of our small town's early years group.

Over the past couple of years I have noticed a growing interest on the part of people across Canada to learn more about *how* to intensify community building to benefit young children. My friend and colleague Tammy and I have taken this as a call to share our experiences, thinking, and passion for the work. I am not an expert in this field . . . and in all of this I remain the little girl of my childhood: asking questions, making connections, and figuring things out as I continue to grow.

TAMMY

By the age of seven I knew that life was fragile, precious, and potentially short. Two events were particularly pivotal for me: My father and mother separated, and shortly after that my family was involved in a tragic car accident. My youngest sister died and my mother spent months in the hospital for surgeries and rehabilitation.

In the wake of the accident, a foster nanny moved into our home to care for me and my remaining two sisters.

What kept me grounded and supported through these upheavals was a sense of community. I was extremely blessed to live in a small town (a rather village-like one). I was surrounded by extended family (grandparents, uncles, aunties, and cousins), friends, and a caring and compassionate larger community. I remember people dropping by with food, or asking me how I was doing when they saw me walking around the neighbourhood. My father and other family members took us camping and snuck us into the hospital for visits to see our mother.

This caring and constant community and family presence taught me to "be there": to be visible in the community and in the lives of other people. Furthermore, experiencing how people can listen and reach out to one another has given me hope. It has inspired in me a vision of the strength that comes when villages are present in the lives of children.

The professional choices I have made as an early childhood educator and human service worker are likely linked to my early experiences. My subsequent career path has revolved on my goal of building a sense of community wherever I find myself. Perhaps it was only natural that I would end up working in a field that puts children first.

ACKNOWLEDGMENTS

It takes a village to write a book! The following individuals have touched our lives, enriching our writing and learning with their engaging stories, supporting materials, personal inspiration, and professional wisdom.

Those who offered written endorsement of the book: Alanna Miller, Anne Graboski, Betty Tate, Carol Munro, Clyde Hertzman, Jim Mustard, Deb Bryant, Denise Robinson, Diane Mayba, Donna March, Joanne Schroeder, John Rampanen, Margaret McGarry, Marian Pickton, Nicki Bezanson, Patti Fraser, Shelley Worthington, Stacey Manson, and Vivian Klassen.

Those who contributed engaging stories and put us on the trail of supportive materials and resources: Aileen Smyth, Andrea Anderson, Brenda Managh, Brenda West, Chris Gay, Esther Pace, Helen Davidson, Jacqueline Smit-Alex, Jameel Rahaman, Marcia Dawson, Mary Gordon, Menno Salvador, Sandi McDonald, Sandy Weeks, Saˇs a Loggin, Susan Foster, Theresa Kingston, and Val Janz.

The social masters: Brynn, Grace, Morgan, Tanner, and their families. Thanks for playing! Warm applause to passionate and skilled early childhood educator Nicki Bezanson. We are in awe of you!

Those who offered their professional wisdom to guide our writing: Thanks to Naomi Pauls of Paper Trail Publishing for creating, from a rough draft of the first chapter, a springboard for the rest of the book, for encouraging us to talk to our readers directly, and for creating a professional book proposal. We greatly appreciate Don Bastian for his interest in our work; his ability to translate our ideas, experiences, and passion into pages; and his publishing wisdom.

The network of Children First and Success by 6® initiatives in British Columbia: You have inspired us with your innovative work. Over the years you have fed our passion with wonderful stories of collaborative journeys, told in conference halls and meeting rooms and over telephone and computer lines.

The people of the Alberni Valley Make Children First Network: Your network is where our real learning occurred. You are generous colleagues and friends who have taught us the practical side of relationship building and collaboration, and what it means to raise a village.

Our families:

TRACY

My thanks to the Townsend and Smyth clans, whose love and support are constant reminders that I have something to share. Mom and Dad, thanks for your unending belief that I can accomplish anything I set my mind to. Connor and Tynan, your special gifts of curiosity and humour feed my soul as a mother. Greg, please accept my gratitude for the original word play on the proverb! Your confidence in me and unwavering patience — as well as our shared vision and values about love, life, and learning — have resulted in this book.

TAMMY

When one works from home, as I often do, a certain amount of flexibility is required from the family. In my case, I am grateful for the liberal doses of patience from my husband and children. Keith, thanks for believing in me and my creative expression. Your humour and quiet understanding are pillars to our family. Curtis and Grace, you are living proof that there is great abundance in this world! You fill me with hope, love, and pride. I appreciate your exclamations of "you will do it, Mom" and for reminding me that everyone sees things differently. You have broadened my thinking and fed my spirit for the writing of this book.

Appreciation goes to my circle of support, the DeClarks, Dewars, Delucias — the family who remind me that home is not always in a "place" but can be found in one another. Time and time again my "go-to-people" in this writing process have been Lynne Delucia (Mom), Bob DeClark (Dad), Al and Judy Dewar, and my siblings (Christine Weir, Debbie DeClark, and Rob DeClark). Thank you for being available to answer questions, to offer perspective or resources, or to care for the kids. I am grounded in gratitude.

*The quality and capacity of
our future population depends
on what we do now
to support early child development.*

— FRASER MUSTARD, FOUNDER,
COUNCIL FOR EARLY CHILD DEVELOPMENT

INTRODUCTION

Who hasn't heard the phrase, "It takes a village to raise a child"? We agree. It does take a village to raise a child. We want to point out, however, that the village itself requires attention and care if it is to uphold its child-raising responsibility.

What does it take to raise the village, then? That is the question we attempt to answer in this book. Raising the village is a concept that aims to build more connections between village members, prompting members of the larger community to take on increased care and responsibility for the well-being of their community.

RAISING THE VILLAGE

Our young century is experiencing a strong global trend to greater community collaboration and greater investment in young children. At a local level, early years community development work surfaces in a number of ways — ways that you may have experienced. Have you attended a local children's fair or event? Perhaps you have a calendar or poster hanging in your office, business, or home highlighting the importance of the first six years in a child's life. Have you ever heard of a local Child and Family Friendly business award? Maybe there is a group of people in your community who meet to discuss and map out early literacy resources for your community. What about public forums on issues affecting children and families, such as the national crisis in child care? These are examples of the tangible outcomes that result when people work together with a focus on children.

To plan and implement such initiatives, it takes a group of committed individuals, organizations, and community members working together to:

- develop collaboratives interested in healthy early child development
- spread the word through community engagement and mobilization
- use research in planning supports and services for children
- jointly create a community plan for early childhood
- advocate for community priorities for young children and families
- allocate funds for locally identified priorities
- evaluate the achievement of local child development outcomes. (Schroeder, 2006)

But why the buzz about the early years in particular? Why are so many communities embarking on this path? Emerging child development research provides compelling arguments that the health and well-being of children are directly linked to brain development in the first six years of life. More than physical health is at stake: Early experiences shape learning, behaviour, and overall health for the rest of a child's life. This in turn shapes our communities and impacts our current and future education, justice, employment, and health-care systems.

The harsh reality is that despite North America's generally high standard of living, one in four children are developmentally vulnerable. They are at risk for the rest of their lives in terms of basic learning, economic participation, social citizenry, and health. Even more startling is the fact that over two hundred million children in the developing world are not reaching their full potential (Irwin, Siddiqi & Hertzman, 2007; McCain, Mustard & Shanker, 2007).

The well-being of children has a complex and interconnected relationship with the well-being of communities. We can all be involved and play a role in defining a child- and family-centred community agenda through collaboration. Every person has the capacity to be a community builder. Parents, grandparents, neighbours, child-care providers, health-care workers, educators, politicians, and entrepreneurs — all contribute because the well-being of children touches us all. For example, early childhood teachers who already demonstrate skilled leadership in their practice with children are well positioned to transfer their strengths outside program walls to further enhance their community. City officials are also well positioned to build community by making policy decisions with a direct impact on young children.

Early years community development is an inclusive, community-driven process that engages people of diverse backgrounds and perspectives to work together to support young children and families. The term "early years community development" was created by Joanne Schroeder in 2006 in her role as advisor for Children First Initiatives in British Columbia, a province-wide government initiative to develop localized systems of service. Early years community development is not a program that delivers a service directly to children; rather, it is a powerful yet accessible means to change the way our world views and serves its children. It builds community connections by understanding the needs of families and fostering innovative ideas to support families with young children.

This targeted form of community development not only influences program opportunities for individual children, it also helps build community capacity and effect policies that will have a positive impact on *many* children. It is big picture: It combines short-term outcomes and long-term planning and embraces the notion that communities can create their own solutions.

Communities and governments often respond to the needs of children and families by implementing initiatives such as anti-bullying programs, language-rich opportunities, gross-motor playtimes, group music for young children, and so on. Such locally driven programs and services are needed and beneficial. However, innovative programs for children are not the *only* way to improve overall outcomes. We suggest a different way to conceptualize community family support: as communities working together to create sustainable approaches both in how they interact and in their goals for serving children. By combining principles of community development with a focus on prevention (more on this below), early years community development becomes an effective vehicle for change.

Simply put, this type of development enables communities to raise the village so the village can raise its children.

COMMUNITY DEVELOPMENT IN A NUTSHELL

It is said that if you give a person a fish, you feed them for a day, whereas if you teach a person how to fish, you feed them for a lifetime. Community development takes this metaphor one step further by encouraging people to ask whether they even want to fish, and, if so, suggesting how they can share their bounty.

Community development is a process that facilitates a community's ability to thrive by empowering both individuals and groups. Building on their strengths, needs, and interests, participants gain the skills needed to effect change in their own communities through collaboration within those communities. By facilitating reflection and action — in an iterative cycle — community development brings individuals of diverse interests together to understand their common purpose.

Originating in eighteenth-century British socialist thinking, community development builds thriving and sustainable communities based on respect and best intentions. It attempts to change typical power structures in a community, removing the barriers that prevent people from participating in the issues that affect their lives. Conversations, meetings, and the sharing of information empower a community to identify its strengths, vulnerabilities, and resources. People who do the work of community development leverage further resources (including economic and political ones) to facilitate change and growth to strengthen communities.

Community development principles can be used to address many different issues, resulting in increased collaboration and thoughtful, relevant community action. Such issues may include seniors, adult literacy, unemployment, homelessness, and tourism or cultural issues. Community development is a lens through which any of a number of social issues can be viewed within a larger context. This book deals in particular with the issue of early child development in the community setting.

PREVENTION: FIXING THE HOLE IN THE BRIDGE

Prevention addresses issues before they become problems. For example, eating nutritious meals, exercising, and quitting smoking are three proven ways to prevent heart disease. Early years community development decreases childhood vulnerabilities by taking advantage of the wide window of opportunity early in children's lives to provide them with the best start possible. This is prevention through neurobiology. "Experiences in early life activate gene expression and result in the formation of critical pathways and processes. Billions of neurons in the brain must be stimulated to form sensing pathways, which influence a person's learning and behaviour, and biological processes which affect physical and mental health" (McCain, Mustard & Shanker, 2007, p. 21).

The following illustrates, as only a fable can, the power of "going upstream" to practice prevention. (Adapted from Cohen, Chavez & Chehimi, 2007.)

While walking along the banks of a river, a passerby notices that someone is drowning. After pulling the person ashore, the rescuer notices another person in the river in need of help. Before long, the river is filled with drowning people, and more rescuers are required to assist the initial rescuer.

At this point, one of the rescuers starts walking upstream.

"Where are you going?" the others ask, annoyed.

"Upstream to see why so many people keep falling into the river in the first place," he replies.

As it turns out, people are falling through a hole in the bridge leading across the river.

The rescuer realizes that unless the hole in the bridge is fixed, rescuers will continue to spend time, energy, and resources trying to save the drowning. Over time, the neglected hole may result in an increase in victims while overtaxing the rescuers.

Prevention is proactive and is aimed at whole populations, not just individuals. It makes good sense because it improves things for everyone while helping those most at risk. As Irwin, Siddiqi & Hertzman have found, "Many challenges in adult society — mental health problems, obesity/stunting, heart disease, criminality, competence in literacy and numeracy — have their roots in early childhood . . . Investment in early childhood is the most powerful investment a country can make, with returns over the life course many times the amount of the original investment" (Irwin et al., 2007, p. 5). Because this type of investment prevents future problems, it is also a responsible way to use public funds. In fact, it is estimated that every dollar spent on early childhood development can save up to $17 in later social costs (Irwin et al., 2007).

Early years community development is the combination of community development and prevention. On the surface, it could be misinterpreted as a children's interest group: "a silo initiative." In her book *Shared Space* (2006), Sherri Torjman expresses concern about emerging initiatives that have in themselves created mini silos within communities, creating ineffective interventions that ultimately force community projects to compete for resources.

The warning is worth heeding. When one attempts to stay grounded in both community development and prevention, there will be times when the wide perspective of early years community development is at the fore and other times when a more focused childhood lens is used. We, for example, have been involved with a number of different community groups that are not focused on young children, such as adult literacy, social responsibility, cultural diversity, community safety, social planning, and municipal budget decisions. However, we can always find a link back to children.

Early years community development has no interest in competing against other initiatives and efforts. It is actually a common thread in *all* of the community issues that present themselves in our complex world. For example, the struggle to decide where to build a new high school brings many issues to the surface, such as intergenerational conflict, environmental concerns, poverty and homelessness, and traffic patterns, not to mention actual educational issues for children and youth. The links to early childhood are present in each and every one of these challenges.

- *Intergenerational conflict* can be reduced and prevented through connecting young children with their elders. As awareness of each group rises, relationships increase understanding and compassion. As the child turns into youth and young adult, the gap narrows and interactions become more tolerant (sometimes even friendly). Youth who are engaged in issues for young children develop positive leadership skills and increase their chances to act as good role models, simultaneously improving relationships between youth and adults. Examples of these efforts include "gran-buddies"; high-school classes partnering with retired builders to construct play apparatus for children; and peer-education programs that connect older students with preschoolers.

• *Environmental efforts* can engage young children. This is important because they will be caretakers of the Earth long after we are gone. Children as young as three or four continue to be the key leaders in recycling awareness and action. Sustainable living is an essential learned behaviour. By starting with an investment in our youngest citizens, we can leverage their capacity to influence their families and strengthen their ability to live gently on our planet as they mature.

• *Poverty and homelessness*—a vicious existence for families—can be addressed. Children are key losers in poverty and a key way to break the cycle. Developing strength and health in all children builds a generation that is more resilient in the face of life's challenges and better able to learn life skills for supporting themselves as productive and happy adults.

• *Traffic patterns*, seemingly far removed from very young children, can be shown to be directly involved. The built environment of a city — including public transit, bicycle lanes, traffic-calm streets, and "human scale architecture" — has an impact on children's health and well-being. Suzanne Crowhurst Lennard (Lennard & Crowhurst-Lennard, 2000), an architect and social advocate, founded the International Making Cities Livable Council. She believes that to make a city livable for all, we must first make it livable for children.

We can learn from these scenarios that a focus on young children is, in fact, a phenomenally effective way to address many complex community issues that may not seem child related on the surface. People involved in early years community development can play a significant role in influencing change and providing both a collaborative and preventative lens for communities as they address complex issues.

Years of practical experience tell us that successful early years community development is relevant, sustainable, and ongoing. It has neither a beginning nor an end. It is collaborative and transformational at the best of times, and messy, complicated, and difficult at the worst.

Early years community development can begin by connecting people with three village-raising strategies:

- building relationships
- framing leadership
- constructing collective relevance.

How do these strategies foster community connections? This book showcases the ramifications of early years community development work through its potential to influence the priorities of communities, organizations, and governments.

PART 1

BRINGING THE VILLAGE TO LIFE

IT TAKES A VILLAGE

"Change will not come if we wait for
some other person or some other time.
We are the ones we've been waiting for.
We are the change that we seek."
— BARACK OBAMA, FROM A CAMPAIGN SPEECH

Let's consider where the saying "it takes a village" comes from and what it means. The source of the proverb is the subject of spirited debate. Its colloquial usage, at least, can be traced back to Africa. That continent boasts a wealth of languages and dialects, and at least three local sayings bear a likeness to the proverb we know in English:

- *Omwana takulila nju emoi:* A child does not grow up only in a single home. — Democratic Republic of Congo

- *Omwana taba womoi:* A child belongs not to one parent or home. — Nigeria

- *Omwana ni wa bhone:* Regardless of a child's biological parent(s), the upbringing belongs to the community. — Tanzania (Mbogoni, 1996)

Similar cultural sayings or traditions are found in societies well beyond Africa. In communities that traditionally use oral storytelling to preserve their culture and teachings, it may not be a phrase per se, but the rituals, traditions, and actions of the people parallel the proverb's meaning.

For example, Tseshaht First Nation elders from the west coast of Vancouver Island recall an important ceremony hosted by the parents of a new baby (Rampanen, 2007). The *imatu~aa*, or Belly Button Ceremony, gathered extended family, friends, and neighbours into a circle. The baby was passed from adult to adult, receiving a precious and individual interaction with each member, whether through a song, a speech, or simply a touch. Each interaction was a resounding statement that the participants would be the baby's lifelong mentors, guides, and guardians. This is a poignant example of a village declaring its love and commitment to raise a child through its cultural teachings and blessings.

A more recent, European example of community organization that embodies the proverb's meaning may be found in the villages surrounding the town of Reggio Emilia in Italy. After World War II, a group of parents spearheaded an innovative preschool that has developed into a philosophy and method of early childhood education. This grassroots, constructivist approach to early education — known as the Reggio Emilia Approach — involves community *and* collaboration. The curriculum originates from the child but is guided and framed by the educator and their shared environment. This approach features a respectful and reciprocal relationship between children, parents, teachers, and community. The many components of a child's world are gathered together to enhance their early years (Rinaldi, 2005). This educational philosophy can be found in Reggio-Emilia-inspired children's centres around the world today.

References to a village-raised child span continents, cultures, and centuries, which suggests just how important a concept it is. Cultural teachings consistently promote the idea that children should receive multiple influences in their early years outside the home that complement the love and support of the nuclear family. If commonality begets importance, it prompts the question: Are these concepts congruent with Western society today, and if so, how do we measure up?

Raising the village sounds like a daunting task. However, although complex and long term, this work is eminently doable when communities begin to work together on issues that support children. However, before reacting to issues with projects and programs, it is best to explore the context. Indeed, getting the big picture will help us move into rich community planning and informed decisions about the actions we should take.

EXPLORING THE ISSUES

Sleeves rolled up, furrowed brows, slumped shoulders, a heaviness in the air . . . Weighed down with an all-consuming sense of responsibility, no one in the room dared pause for so much as a coffee break. The participants were focused, intense, and determined to wade through the fog and confusion.

In front of each chair was a stack of papers bursting with negative statistics and cold statements about the well-being of children in the community. On the one hand, the documents held great validity and interest for those around the table. On the other hand, the information they bore failed to reflect the spirit of the community or the hard work that this group and others had dedicated to children and families. The overwhelming task before them was to make sense of the data, define the key issues, and make a plan to better meet the needs of the community.

Sound familiar? Although the issues will vary, this situation is common to many communities, groups, and organizations. Local problems of bullying, crime, poverty, child abuse, environmental concerns, and obesity can all spur concerned discussions. There is great value in *not* rushing through these conversations and exploring issues instead through dialogue — what we call "unearthing." Benefits of unearthing include:

- an informed final outcome — one that people feel connected to
- a richness that goes deeper than surface reactions
- a process that honours and draws on the multiple strengths of many stakeholders.

It is critical for communities to launch their own process of discovery, to find what works for them, and then to create a shared understanding of the issues that emerge. As Blaise Pascal, the French mathematician and philosopher of the sixteenth century, said, "People are generally better persuaded by the reasons they have discovered themselves than by those which have come in to the minds of others" (Pascal, 2007, p. 11).

What did it take to move forward in the case of the heavy-aired boardroom? What did this group need to move from the seemingly insurmountable issues they faced to a plan of action? Perseverance, hope, and a can-do attitude helped. So did their belief that uncovering a process to guide them through the murky, complex data would help them emerge feeling informed and ready to make suggestions about what, if anything, should be done. This group spent six months expressing, sharing, and learning before they were ready to act. Meetings included time to vent frustrations and feelings about the hard realities, to listen to other points of view, and to ask questions, leading to an ever-deeper process of discovery.

ISSUES ON THE TABLE

Here are some of the hot issues in early years community development as reported at a Canadian conference on this work in 2008:

- finding a way to reach vulnerable children and their families

- addressing the unique challenges of working in rural and isolated communities
- figuring out how to advance the child-care agenda
- ensuring that all basic needs are met (housing, sleep, food, clothing)
- honouring the unique status of Aboriginal people and their perspectives on community and children's development
- understanding the impacts of poverty, literacy, and immigration on child development
- securing new and sustainable funding based on community strategic plans
- listening to parents
- building on the strengths of parents and caregivers.

FINDING THE TOOLS

Expressing, sharing, and learning are the key activities that enable groups to gain context and an increased understanding of the many variables and issues affecting complex social situations. A seemingly overwhelming issue can be unpacked into manageable chunks by using readily available "tools" or processes, including:

- listening to stakeholders
- learning from research and literature
- exposing attitudes and values.

In our facilitation experience with groups, we have used these tools to unearth many of the issues that arise in early years community development.

LISTENING TO STAKEHOLDERS

Focus groups, surveys, and public forums are a few examples of ways to listen to stakeholders — locally, nationally, or even internationally. In 2007, more than seven hundred and fifty parents from all over British

Columbia participated in a telephone survey about their experiences as parents today. The B.C. Council for the Family conducted the survey with the goal of increasing the provincial understanding of parents' attitudes toward their roles, their children, and parenting in today's world. The questions examined issues ranging from the type of information parents seek to gain from parenting classes to the effect of media on society and to parents' hopes and dreams for their children. Here are some of the survey's findings:

- 75% of the parents surveyed were employed outside the home, either full or part time.
- 56% of the households were traditional nuclear families (two parents plus at least one child), 21% were single-parent families, 11% were multigenerational, 5% were step families, and 1% were foster families.
- 50% of the working parents surveyed reported having employers with policies that support parenting.
- 80% of the parents surveyed reported using Web-based parenting resources and admitted that they were not always diligent in evaluating the quality of the Websites.
- 67% of respondents were unable to name any public figure who was an appropriate role model for parents.
- 75% of the parents surveyed believed their children have more opportunities than they had as children.
- 66% believed their children are more supervised than they were when they were children.
- 41% indicated they do not have enough time for parenting.

Listening to stakeholders opens access to interesting and diverse perspectives that may validate or challenge the current understanding of an issue. Unearthing their views helps give voice to groups that otherwise may not have a voice in community planning. We can unearth further by asking ourselves the following questions:

- Are the results expected or surprising?
- What picture do they create about the stakeholders (in this case, parents in B.C.)?
- What else needs to be explored?
- How applicable are these results to other areas or other groups?

THE PARENTS' PERSPECTIVE

Participants in the B.C. parent survey commented on the best things about being a parent. These included:

- Allowing a child to grow and develop into a wonderful person.
- Seeing what kind of person you can help them be.
- Being a part of their lives.
- Having an impact on someone else's life.
- Having someone who loves you as much as you love them.
- Being childlike with them.
- Doing fun things with children when they're younger.
- Being part of a family.
- Children make us better people.
- With children, all things become meaningful.

LEARNING FROM RESEARCH AND LITERATURE

Analysing and discussing statistics, books, papers, and practice-based study outcomes are all ways to learn from research and literature. Hard facts help clarify child development issues in a way that is not biased with perceptions, assumptions, and political agendas. In fact, statistics help set responsive and responsible agendas that address real issues and needs effectively. The use of research can play a significant role in convincing government and policy makers that young children and families are an important social agenda. Action is needed, and citing evidence that child vulnerability exists helps those committed to creating a positive future to find support. Alfredo Solari, a senior health advisor with the Inter-American Development Bank, wisely warns: "No data, no problem, no action."

On the forefront of early child development research is a Canadian organization, the Human Early Learning Partnership, or HELP for short. HELP is an interdisciplinary research unit with connections to six universities in British Columbia and international partnerships and research connections in countries including Australia, Switzerland, the United States, Holland, and the United Kingdom.

In 2005, HELP was designated the Global Knowledge Hub for Early Child Development by the World Health Organization. HELP produces a treasure trove of solid, evidence-based knowledge and has emerged as a global leader in early child development research and monitoring from a population-health perspective. It is an invaluable resource to early years community developers trying to bridge the gap between the science behind early childhood and the action needed at local levels. Their vision to create, promote, and apply new knowledge to help children thrive is reflected in the accessibility of their knowledge for communities through their staff and Website (earlylearning.ubc.ca).

The flagship research unit for HELP is the Early Child Development Mapping Project, which brings together academic, government, and community partners to work together to better understand children's development at the level of the population. The project uses a standardized tool called the EDI (Early Development Instrument) to measure and then geographically map out child vulnerability in the areas of social and emotional well-being, language and cognitive development, communication, and physical health. The results of the EDI "represent the outcome of the cumulative early experience that children in a given geographic area have had from birth to kindergarten" (Hertzman & Irwin, 2007, p. 2).

Since initiating a province-wide data collection in British Columbia (now performed annually), HELP has been able to demonstrate—with valid data — the justifiability of investing in children. The results are fascinating and useful. Thanks to this groundbreaking work, B.C. has experienced an elevated awareness of the importance of the early years, and this is being reflected in political will, policies, and funding priorities. This Canadian province still has a long journey ahead of it to demonstrate improved outcomes for children and their families, but without a doubt the data have initiated a push in the right direction.

In addition to changes at the political level, the EDI data help local communities develop practical ways to support children given the challenges faced by families, schools, and communities. This information provides specific insight about the neighbourhoods where families live and the domains of development that show the greatest vulnerability. The EDI gives early years community developers one piece of the complex puzzle of what influences the lives of children.

Whether your community has access to local EDI data or not, you can learn much from the trends emerging from this research throughout British Columbia, across Canada, and around the world. In addition, consider other research tools that your community can access. What kinds of data are available to help you understand the full context of the world in which children live? How can local knowledge be used to determine the kind of data to be collected? How can information about child vulnerability influence program decisions, policy, and community attitudes toward early child development?

Learning from perspectives outside the early childhood field can also be helpful to develop a fuller understanding of the context in which children grow. In their book *Kidfluence*, Anne Sutherland and Beth Thompson (2001) describe the role children play in today's economically driven society. They also describe the tension that is generated between the values that reflect the good old days and the outlook for the future. Their belief is that children are experiencing a changed role in response to our shifting society. Their examples include:

- Parents today value their kids' opinions and take them into consideration when making decisions that affect the whole family.
- Children today mean "big business." They participate in many decisions that affect families, including grocery shopping, travel, entertainment, and media. They represent a large and important target audience for advertisers.
- Children today receive a seemingly mixed message to grow up faster and to preserve their youth. (The authors argue that this reflects an evolutionary step toward achieving balance.)

With such information in hand, we can dig deeper, asking such questions as: What are the pros and cons of children's roles in today's economy? What are the implications of consumerism and marketing? Is it useful to examine differences between generations? What could this tell us? What is the role of communities in supporting the balance between progress and tradition?

Keep exploring many sources. Documentaries, podcasts, and numerous written resources are available to expand learning. A few of the authors who have inspired us to challenge our own assumptions about children, families, and society include Barbara Coloroso, Barry MacDonald, Carl Dunst, David Elkind, Gordon Neufeld, Jennifer Fox, Mary Gordon, and Michael Ungar.

EXPOSING ATTITUDES AND VALUES

Techniques to expose attitudes and values include personal reflection, group dialogue, and community observation. As authors, mothers, and community developers, we examined our values about the role of children and families in our society through a process of self-reflection, brainstorming, and dialogue. Here's what we discovered.

First, we believe that children are competent, contributing members of society. Children are interesting and very complex. They embody many paradoxes that, as adults, we need to acknowledge and celebrate.

They are strong, full, and complete beings and at the same time are vulnerable and dependent on love and guidance for their well-being and for their development.

Second, we do not subscribe to the viewpoint that children are empty vessels at birth that are "filled" by adults. Rather, we strongly believe that children are co-constructors of both themselves and their community. They are natural creators with the courage, determination, and tenacity required to both take care of our world and change it. Our role is to foster the potential of their genius and stay out of their way.

Third, we celebrate families' social, cultural, and spiritual diversity as well as their differences in structure. We respect the uniqueness of individual families while we search for the synergy that is created when we realize our common bonds.

Dig even deeper by asking yourself how *you* view children and families. How can shared values advance community collaboration? How can opposing values still hold meaning in community collaboration? Look around at the richness of families. How do families "show up" and how do you see them treated?

Listening to stakeholders, learning from research and literature, and exposing attitudes and values are three manageable and meaningful tools for deconstructing complex topics. The tools provide opportunities through exploratory conversations to develop both a common understanding of the issues and a common language to talk about them. Professional lingo, acronyms, and even widely known sayings — in our case, "it takes a village to raise a child" — often require clarification. In fact, as we developed our ideas while writing this book, we realized that the terms "village" and "community" had become interchangeable jargon words. We felt that the terms needed to be disentangled for a better understanding of the familiar proverb.

DEFINING THE VILLAGE

*"A community of completely independent
people is not a community at all."*
— MARY GORDON, *ROOTS OF EMPATHY*

I t takes a village to raise a child. It takes a community to raise a
child. So what exactly is the difference between a village and a
community?

We define community as a group of people sharing some kind of
commonality, such as culture, employer, neighbourhood, interests, or
philosophy. Individuals are connected to many communities simultaneously. (See diagram.)

OUR MANY COMMUNITIES

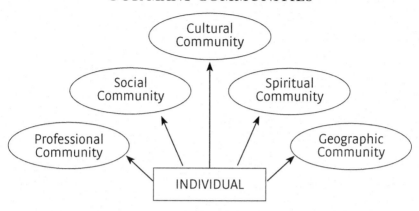

We define village, on the other hand, as not one but multiple communities that are building connections. How each village looks will be different in every location. In fact, how they look *must* be different, because villages draw on the unique strengths and resources of those involved. (See diagram.)

ONE VILLAGE, MANY COMMUNITIES

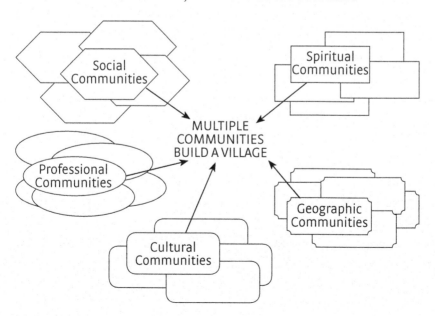

Is there a list of people and places that every village must have in order to be functional? If you have schools, churches, hospitals, police officers, municipal politicians, and a fire hall, does that make your community a village? Must the list in one location be equal to that in another for a village to have the ingredients to thrive? The answers are no, no, and no.

Although public brick and mortar and a variety of services are critical to a community's ability to serve its population, another factor is essential: "social capital," the ways in which our lives are made more productive by social connections. In his provocative book *Bowling Alone*, Robert Putnam explores changes in social and civic engagement in the United States, explaining the consequences of reduced social capital. He states that "child development is powerfully shaped by social capital . . . [which] keeps bad things from happening to good kids" (Putnam, 2000, p. 296).

Putnam cites research suggesting that the level of informal social capital (such as families visiting with friends, card games, and other casual social recreation) is more closely correlated to school success than formal community interactions, such as club meetings, church attendance, and planned community programs and projects. This indicates that there is "something about communities," when people connect with one another, that positively affects the development of children. In other words, people enhance the capacity of each other's success through friendships, social time, and generally being engaged.

This is the village we want to create for the benefit of all children. Paul Kershaw writes, "Like the African proverb, 'It takes a village to raise a child,' the social care concept implies that the community context in which children and other citizens mature influences their development. Put simply, the assumption is that the village nurtures" (Kershaw, 2009, para. 3).

Our book explores the concept of the village through three village-raising strategies — building relationships, framing leadership, and constructing collective relevance — to help build the connections within and between communities. When sustained, these connections support community collaboration, better opportunities, and ultimately better outcomes for children. Following is an overview of the three strategies, each of which will be developed further in subsequent chapters.

STRATEGY #1 / BUILDING RELATIONSHIPS: ESTABLISHING CONNECTIONS

People are the defining force of a village. Magic happens when people interact and communicate, directly influencing direction, momentum, and commitment to action. Think about it: Do things get done behind closed doors at a policy level or do they happen as a result of informal conversations — or both? For example, could fried onions, ketchup, and a counter full of warm buns be a valid scene for building relationships for community success? Anything is possible! When we wish to begin or build on early years community development, we need to look at all interactions as opportunities. (See sidebar below.)

The success of a small-town annual community celebration is fundamentally the result of relationships between people. No matter where the connections happen, possibilities exist. The energy created by human interactions is one element contributing to the characteristics of a village. When people gather around an issue, social capital is strengthened. The group evolves to achieve a common understanding, and individuals working together benefit from seeing issues through multiple perspectives.

LIGHTING UP A COMMUNITY

Streaks of spilled mustard and ketchup on top of a picnic table create an artist's masterpiece. Where better to catch the pulse of a community than at a volunteer hot dog stand?

The mayor orders up a double frank with the works. As he waits, he discusses the changing economy and the difficulties of encouraging people to stay in town.

Next in line is Mr. Arthur, a local businessperson, who states, "We have to do something about the deteriorating downtown core — revitalization is what this town needs."

Mrs. Dawson hurries over for some ice-cream cones to cool off her family. "We need more things for our children to do," she says.

Dozens and dozens of opinions, thoughts, feelings, and perspectives are shared at the hot dog stand.

The volunteer cashier and the onion fryer huddle over coffee at the end of their shift to unwind and talk over their busy day. As they debrief, a theme begins to arise from the day's comments. An hour later the two have sketched their plan on a napkin. They will propose a festival of lights to showcase the spirit of the community.

Starting with fifty-odd strings of lights and a few pole decorations for the downtown core, a festival takes shape. Residents are inspired to participate in a community event while being encouraged to support local merchants. At the town square in the pouring rain on the night in question, organizers are doubtful that the event will get off the ground.

Surprise! Over nine hundred people show up with their umbrellas, singing carols, carrying candles, and applauding as the new lights are turned on. Volunteers man free hot chocolate booths while popcorn machines and hot dog stands are in full swing.

The community seems to want this festival to succeed ...

As the years pass, more and more people offer their services and expertise to help out. The senior citizens stage "screwin' in the light bulb" parties and supply hot lunches for other volunteers working to decorate the town.

The festival grows and by year ten the town has over ten thousand people coming to enjoy the evening's events (thousands of them come from outside the community). Over 150,000 lights now twinkle and decorations abound. Organizers are awed by the positive actions and dedication of the volunteers.

STRATEGY #2 / FRAMING LEADERSHIP: STRENGTHENING CONNECTIONS

"The world is run by people who show up," says a popular bumper sticker. It's these people, the ones who give of their time, who are the movers and shakers — the real leaders. As a concept, leadership is hard to define. Too often we confuse it with the person leading. But leadership can be found anywhere and in anyone. It can be found at city hall, in the grocery store, at a Native friendship centre, or on the school playground.

Many authors have attempted to define leadership. Here are some of our favourite definitions:

- "Leadership is a relationship between those who aspire to lead and those who choose to follow" (Kouzes & Pozner, 2002, p. 24).
- "When the effective leader is finished with his work, the people say it happened naturally" (Lao Tse, 650 BC).
- ". . . leadership starts as a feeling, a desire to serve others that then becomes a commitment to move that desire into practice" (Wheatley, 1999, para. 9).
- "A leader is the one who climbs the tallest tree, surveys the entire situation and yells, 'Wrong jungle!'" (Covey, 2004, p. 101).

Although we traditionally associate leadership with authority, true leadership is demonstrated through skill in developing shared values, including all voices, empowering others, and ultimately respecting the relationships that people already hold. This can be accomplished by leveraging the leadership that already exists within a group.

Leadership is manifested when individuals offer their strengths to a collaborative effort. This may include creating harmony among competitive organizations, considering the possible implications of new ideas, or envisioning a big and bright future. What other forms can leadership take? Here are just a few: leading by example, quietly getting the job done, standing up to motivate and encourage others, boldly taking on big projects, and enthusiastically fostering teamwork.

Early years community development work is typically not a person's main focus. Often it is something they do off the side of their desks. Having a person dedicated to facilitate and move forward the work of a collaborative means that the job *is* their desk, freeing others to participate fully and making the most of their contributions. The way we see it, leadership does not fall to traditional decision makers only. In early years community development, everyone can play an important role in how children are supported. A balance of group leadership and facilitative leadership, against the backdrop of formal and informal structures, can make it happen.

STRATEGY #3 / CONSTRUCTING COLLECTIVE RELEVANCE: SEEING THE CONNECTIONS

The key question we ask when we look at community collaborative work is, "What is the connection for people and their organizations?" The answer is relevance.

Exploring both personal and organizational relevance helps communities learn why people participate in community development work, why they stay, and what keeps the momentum going. Knowing this encourages the collaborative to seek out and harness the strengths within the group and encourages people to be mindful of what they have to offer. *Raising the Village* introduces "collective relevance" as a new term to describe the possibilities that exist in the power of collaboration.

Each person has reasons for participating in any community activity or organized committee. They may be motivated by their passion for change, have particular strengths they want to contribute, be driven by their personal interests, or a combination of all of these things. This is *personal relevance.*

In addition, if a person represents a larger group, such as a workplace or social club, or even an ethnic group or neighbourhood, they will also be reflecting the passion, strengths, and interests of the larger group. This is *organizational relevance.*

Collective relevance creates a synergy in which people see how community collaborative efforts go *beyond* shared values, shared stakes, shared visions, and shared action. This higher level of relevance draws from both personal and organizational relevance to create something new and unifying that the collaborative builds together.

Consider participation in the environmental movement, for example. What began as activism from a minority group of environmentalists in the 1960s has stepped onto an international stage, giving environmental topics and issues a greater relevance in our world and making everyone from government policy-makers to individual homeowners aware of the issues. Simply put, people are starting to change their attitudes because they now see the connection between their actions and saving the Earth.

Collective relevance and the synergy it creates can be seen in a group of children planting trees, composting, or working with a municipal government to create "idle free" zones. Children, families, organizations, and communities are on the verge of making the connection between their participation, contributions, strengths, and something larger than themselves. A focus on children, like a focus on the environment, has the potential to change our world, one village at a time.

WHAT THE SOCIAL
MASTERS SAY

*"A master in the art of living draws
no sharp distinction between his work and his play,
his labour and his leisure, his mind and his body,
his education and his recreation.
He hardly knows which is which. He simply
pursues his vision of excellence through
whatever he is doing and leaves others
to determine whether he is working or playing."*
— L.P. JACKS, *EDUCATION THROUGH RECREATION*

How do we bring our definition of village alive? How do we apply the village-raising strategies of building relationships, framing leadership, and constructing collective relevance to form collaborative partnerships? For answers, we went to "the source," a small group of social-networking gurus, absolute masters of their trade, and observed them building a village from the ground up.

What you take and absorb from this observed activity is entirely personal. To us, the interactions between the children speak volumes about the process of "unearthing the village," providing a practical example of how communities interact and begin forming connections with one another.

How the children's village develops, grows, and changes over time can be compared with early years community development. Follow the children and early childhood educator in this chapter and throughout the book and watch as they build relationships, frame leadership, and construct collective relevance.

ONE SMALL VILLAGE

Meet our expert social masters: Tanner (age five), Morgan (four), and Grace and Brynn (both almost three years old). An early childhood educator joins them to observe and encourage them in their spontaneous village building.

They start with a bag filled with large foam blocks: the stimuli. The four preschool participants have assumed the role of land surveyors or village engineers, extracting the shapes and colours of their choice. They become acquainted with the textures of the blocks by rolling, twirling, and hoisting each building piece. They work in unison to empty the bag, then quickly retreat to four separate corners of the living room to begin their parallel play. The children are eager to converse with the educator but say little to each other.

For two minutes they busily stack their individual structures until Tanner announces that he has built a *big* castle. Grace compares her structure of blocks to Tanner's and states that hers is a *small* castle. They compare momentarily, then carry on in their separate spaces.

About a minute later we hear Brynn exclaim, "Hey!" The top two blocks of her structure have fallen to the carpet. The educator offers a prompt to the room: "What can we do?" But she barely gets the words out before Grace leaves her building to join Brynn. The two of them work together to place the blocks back on top of the structure.

Morgan is watching this interaction with raised eyebrows. She lurches forward as if to join in, then sits back in front of her blocks. The educator notices this movement. "Morgan, would you like to add a block, too?" she asks.

Morgan nods her agreement and stands up to help. However, Brynn's entire structure has now fallen to the floor.

Tanner notices the group gathering in front of the fallen blocks and suggests with enthusiasm, "Can we build a big castle that we can all go in?"

Morgan, Grace, and Brynn start working together to build a tall structure. Meanwhile Tanner breaks down his own block structure, offering his pieces to make the group creation larger.

Ask yourself:

- What brings the children together? What's behind *your* reasons for working with others?

- Group work often begins with people working in their independent silos. In the description above, is that how the children worked? Are there lessons here for moving out of our silos?

- Blocks will fall in early years community development. How do our social masters react when this happens?

It is often difficult to distinguish between work and play. In the above observation, they are completely interconnected. We encourage you to look at the complex work of early years community development through the lens of play — to stop and consider what constitutes non-urgent but important work and what might be holding you back from blending the two.

NON-URGENT BUT IMPORTANT WORK

All communities have unique characteristics, strengths, and resources. And their members also have a wide range of world views, agendas, and priorities. Early years community development offers strategies to navigate the complexities of children, families, and communities. The three village-raising strategies we propose, although discussed in the following chapters in a sequential fashion, are not linear. Communities will find that, at any stage of community development, a strategy may resurface with a different twist, a new challenge, and fresh possibilities.

As individuals who have participated in and facilitated an early years collaborative for over a decade, we can say from experience that this work can be isolating, challenging, and ever changing. Even the most seasoned early years community developer will still be faced with situations that benefit from innovative thinking and new skills as well as support from a community of practice. Whether you are new to this work or not, and whatever role you play in an early years community, regular reflection on how relationships, leadership, and relevance play a part in your work will prove a powerful platform for professional and personal development.

In part 2 we will narrow the focus to building relationships. For now, let us offer three activities that are designed to help your early years community unearth the meaning of "raising the village." Our hope is that these and the further activities sprinkled throughout the book will provide a guide, or a starting point, to encourage personal and collective dialogue that can spark new insights and inspiration. Too often we schedule time for urgent work (crisis reactions, budgets, and external demands) but neglect to take time out for non-urgent but important work (professional development, personal growth, and interactive activities). In our experience, when these activities are incorporated into meetings and facilitated in an environment conducive to openness and deep sharing, they help the group get to the heart of working together.

Adapt, add, and edit the activity suggestions to fit you and your community and ignite strong, meaningful conversations. Make time to look within and look without. See what you discover. Have fun.

ACTIVITY #1

ENVISIONING A VILLAGE

General Idea

Influenced by Appreciative Inquiry (AI), this activity helps participants to unearth the best parts of their "village" and carry this image forward for future collaboration with others. The activity takes a group through the first two stages of AI: discovery and dream.

What's Worked for Us . . .

STEP 1

Find a positive story.

When you hear the word "village," what comes to mind? Take a few moments to visualize the village you grew up in. Dig deep into your memory to access your fondest associations and experiences.

> Consider the following questions as you think about your childhood "village":
>
> • Who was there?
>
> • What were your traditions?
>
> • What extended family, friends, or adults embraced you?
>
> • What parts of your neighbourhood felt good?
>
> • Did you have spiritual connections?
>
> • Where did you feel safe and supported?
>
> • What values did your "village" communicate to you as a child?

STEP 2

Discover strengths and successes to build on.

With a partner or in a small group, share a story that illustrates the positive experiences from your past. Describe the circumstances that made this possible. Write down the highlights of each individual's experience and find the common threads or themes of success. Find examples of the most meaningful memories.

STEP 3

Dream what could be.

Drawing on the common themes identified in step 2, dream and share as a group your ideas about what could be. Write a statement that describes an ideal future for children or society, marrying the past and the present as if it were already here. Celebrate the diversity of the past experiences we bring to the table and the common themes of success that link us together. *What have you learned about one another?*

ACTIVITY #2

DRILLING DOWN BENEATH THE FACTS

General Idea

Based on a technique called The 5 Whys, this group activity will extract the maximum amount of information from a simple fact. The technique parallels the way children learn about their environment by asking a stream of questions.

Reawaken your curiosity. Starting with a fact, ask the question "Why?" over and over. Each answer will uncover a new level of inquiry.

What's Worked for Us . . .

STEP 1

Choose a fact.

This could be related to a topic that the group is trying to better understand or it could be a piece of research or evaluation data.

STEP 2

Ask why.

Using a whiteboard or flip-chart paper, record the fact and start asking *why?*

STEP3

Sort the record.

When the whys have been exhausted, sort the record. There will be items the group may choose to investigate further, items that call for action planning, or items that need to be delegated to somebody else.

Here's an example to get you started:

Fact: Licensed Child-care Centre X is closing.

Why? They don't have enough staff.

Why? There are not enough people trained in early childhood education in the community.

Why? Colleges are not attracting enough people to take this certification.

Why? Early childhood educator wages are very low.

Why? The profession is undervalued.

You can see how this exercise broadens the context of a simple fact. It helps you "connect the dots" and root out causes as well as possible solutions.

ACTIVITY #3

NEWSPAPER SEARCH

General Idea

This activity, performed in a group or on your own, helps demonstrate how even seemingly unrelated topics are connected to the early years. The process may help broaden perspectives, find new partners for collaboration, and potentially drum up some innovative community action.

What's Worked for Us . . .

STEP 1

Provide small groups with a copy of a newspaper.

This could be different sections of one big paper, or the main section of several different newspapers. Consider local papers, big city papers, or even foreign papers.

STEP 2

Instruct the small groups to review the articles and find a connection to early years in every article.

They could cut and paste the articles out on flip-chart paper along with their connecting points or they could use markers to write directly on the paper.

STEP 3

Share with the larger group.

Ask: What is going on in the news that provides a different perspective on the early years? Do common themes emerge from this activity?

PART 2

BUILDING RELATIONSHIPS

GETTING SOMETHING DONE

"Knowing is not enough; we must apply.
Willing is not enough; we must do."
— GOETHE

How many early years community developers does it take to replace a light bulb? Lots! One group to research the benefits and implications of said light bulb; one group to do a media campaign about the importance of changing a light bulb; one group to raise money to pay for the light bulb; one group (of course) to do the actual work; and a final group to do an extensive evaluation of the process and outcome.

The catch is that if they don't talk to one another and collaborate, nothing will actually get done. The report on benefits and implications will collect dust on the shelf, the media campaign won't have information to engage public support, funding will not be available to pay for the light bulb, and, alas, no light bulb will be replaced.

Joking aside, there is power in doing a job collaboratively, whether the task is simple or complex.

COLLABORATING

At its most basic level, collaboration is a process by which people approach problems or shared interests as a group and actively seek a mutually determined course of action. The intention of collaboration is to create an appreciation of an issue that is more comprehensive than any singular stakeholder could construct alone.

For this to be successful, stakeholders must recognize that on their own they have an incomplete appreciation of an issue and a limited vision of what can be achieved. Collaboration is a unique process that facilitates a vision of a complete, fully integrated project beyond pilot projects and single systems. The power is in joining differing perspectives to address a common issue. This process can build bridges between organizations and between organizations and the communities in which they serve. In turn this results in tangible outcomes and an increased ability to meet future challenges. The lingo for this is *community capacity*.

Ask anyone who has worked in the early childhood education field for ten years or more and they will tell you that this sector has been engaged in an uphill battle of professional advocacy since the 1940s. In Canada, a change in federal government in 2006 culminated in the rejection of a national child-care plan that had been carefully and consistently developed by professionals. The new government had different plans and philosophies, and the early child education field and child-care practitioners landed back at square one: being undervalued for the work they do with young children. Constituencies in the sector took an emotional hit, many of them deflating like a flat tire.

This time, however, support came from others who were incensed with the lack of change: from people who weren't child-care practitioners or early child educators. These new advocates could see that the sector was ready to give up the ghost.

Cities held community rallies and town-hall meetings. In one community, a gathering drew in over seventy people, 75% of whom were not from the child-care sector. They were nurses, school district representatives, municipal politicians, parents, and entrepreneurs. The participants looked around and noted two things. One was the deplorable lack of value that Canada was placing on the child-care sector. The other was that the sector itself was not strong enough to continue under another half century of oppression.

The group recommended working locally to strengthen the sector by building the profession. They identified a leader and created a paid position using funds earmarked for early years community development. Over the next two years, bonds between people in the sector were developed, feelings of self-value and worth were increased, and broad connections within the community were systematically strengthened. The result: an increased ability to respond as a cohesive group.

Collaboration occurs for a variety of reasons. It may be induced by conflict or born from a shared interest (Corbett, 2002; Gray, 1989). Stakeholders recognize the potential advantages of working together on early childhood issues. Collaboration induced from a shared interest is intentional in nature; it embraces possibilities and focuses passions in a way that goes beyond merely "solving a problem." The famous parable by Loren Eiseley (1979) called "The Starfish Story," paraphrased below, poignantly illustrates the importance of working with purpose.

One day a man was walking along the beach when he noticed a boy picking something up and gently throwing it into the ocean. Approaching the boy, he asked, "What are you doing?"

"Throwing starfish back into the ocean," the youth replied. "The surf is up and the tide is going out. If I don't throw them back, they'll die."

"Son," the man said, "don't you realize there are miles and miles of beach and hundreds of starfish? You can't make a difference!"

After listening politely, the boy bent down, picked up another starfish, and threw it back into the surf. Then, smiling at the man, he said, "I made a difference for that one."

The young boy in the story is acting with focus, purpose, and passion. He is armed with the knowledge that he is making an important difference — one starfish at a time. Allow us to add a playful twist to this story to illustrate the value both of individual efforts and a broader community picture.

To understand the early years community development approach, picture the beach full of people each throwing starfish back to safety and collectively making a significant impact on the survival of the starfish population. They are united in purpose and passion and have found ways to work together so that there is some semblance of process and order. People aren't just randomly tossing starfish; they ensure that the starfish don't collide in the air, they communicate to one another about how fast the ocean is receding, and they cheer one another on as each wave crashes in.

The parallels between this parable and serving a population of children are many. We see individuals and organizations doing important work, one child at a time. We also see how powerful this effort is when joined with that of many others. In other words, early years community development is not intended to replace or displace the attention and care given by parents, service providers, or organizations that serve individual children. It is intended to coordinate efforts so that the outcome can be broader and many children and even whole societies can benefit.

COLLABORATIVES

In the world of early years community development, groups of people are the movers and shakers in improving community conditions and increasing opportunities for children. Across Canada, throughout the US, and across the ocean, these groups of people are called many things: networks, coalitions, committees, groups, or tables. The umbrella term and most descriptive name for them is "collaboratives." This indicates both the nature of the work and the level of integration sought. More than an interagency group, a collaborative in early years community development is a multi-stakeholder shared venture — and adventure.

ONE CREATION STORY

Where do communities begin when it comes to this type of collaboration? A common group creation story looks something like the following.

Every second Wednesday morning from nine to twelve a local child and youth committee huddles in an available office space to network and connect. On the plus side, this meeting represents one of the only networking opportunities for this community group of dedicated social service providers. On the minus side, the mandates and interests of the participants are so incredibly broad and varied that nothing beyond social networking occurs.

The group struggles with how to organize itself and find a common focus and direction. The volunteer facilitators — graciously doing the work off the sides of their desks — decide to divide the group into three subcommittees according to their target age groups: prenatal to six years, six to twelve years, and twelve to eighteen years.

This restructuring revitalizes those passionate about the issues for very young children. The participants in this subcommittee immediately begin to pursue deepened, specific, and meaningful conversations. Their shared issues, early years experience, and focused dialogue result in enthused interactions.

Momentum grows and with it a discovery that their drive and capacity for making community change and having community impact surpasses that of the rest of the child and youth committee. Soon the prenatal to age six group explodes with a life of its own, becoming autonomous of the original committee.

Collaboratives have potential to have a profound impact on the village. There are many possibilities and opportunities to get the work done when you have a group. Collaboratives are filled with people who can connect with one another and form meaningful relationships. It is one thing to create a space to bring diverse people together to meet and work on early years issues. It is quite another to intentionally build relationships so that each person feels a part of the collaborative. "A purposeful group is not just a collection of individuals. A group is an entity in itself" (Hunter, Bailey & Taylor, 1995, p. 31).

COLLABORATIVES:

- save money and other resources
- achieve more than any single organization
- have a greater combined sphere of influence than one organization
- have greater credibility than a single organization
- provide an opportunity to share information
- increase access to target populations
- increase access to additional resources
- encourage cooperation and collaboration.

WHO THE WHO IS

*"Children are one third of our population
and all of our future."*
— SELECT PANEL FOR THE PROMOTION OF CHILD HEALTH (1981)

One of the first (and ongoing) tasks in community collaboration is figuring out *who* the who is.

Stop! Do not dare think you can skip this section! Those of you involved with long-term, established collaboratives or networks may be feeling a little tempted to thumb past these pages because, after all, you have all the right people at the table, so why not get on with it?

Double stop! Challenge the way you look at participation. Has your membership changed, evolved, and grown to its greatest potential? Is there room for new, outside-the-box discussions with community? Are there undercurrents of power and territory struggles? For collaboratives to be effective, consideration of the nature of participation must be an ongoing effort. The way individuals will be involved in the collaborative is not a one-shot deal to be discussed only at the startup or beginning stages. It must be looked at on many levels throughout all stages of development.

When it comes to participation, there are the "usual suspects" who live and work directly with young children, and then there are the non-traditional partners who have a formative, albeit indirect, influence on the big picture of children in communities. First ask the question, Who makes up my village?

The centre of a village includes:

- children
- parents
- grandparents
- extended family
- foster parents
- friends and neighbours.

Surrounding the centre are those who develop or run programs that are offered to families with young children, such as:

- child-care providers
- preschool teachers
- teachers and administrators of schools
- nurses
- midwives and doulas
- nutritionists
- dental professionals
- doctors and pediatricians
- those trained to support families with children with extra needs
- social workers
- housing and social assistance workers
- librarians
- family support workers
- spiritual leaders

- counsellors at women's and men's centres
- mental health clinicians
- volunteers (e.g., retired professionals).

There are also organizations that support a bigger infrastructure where the needs of children are (or should be) considered, including:
- parks and recreation (swimming, skating, camps, etc.)
- organizations that support families living in poverty (social services, soup kitchens, employment assistance)
- colleges and universities (faculty, programs, and research)
- arts communities
- faith communities (churches)
- multicultural associations
- senior organizations
- volunteer bureaus
- employment and career centres
- municipal governments (city councillors, police, fire, city maintenance, planners)
- Chambers of Commerce or other economic development organizations
- major employers (health, education, industry)
- real estate agencies
- small local businesses
- large retail chains.

This list may look long and intimidating. The reality is that not everyone will be engaged at the same time or in the same way. The list is meant to be a starting point and is not exhaustive (though it may be exhausting). There will be differences in urban and rural settings, in where you are in the world, and in how mobilized and aware your community is of local early child development issues. It is both a place to start and a place to broaden how you might think about someone who has something to offer.

THE MANY SPHERES OF INFLUENCE

When thinking about engaging organizations in this work, it can be unclear at what level to direct your efforts: toward front-line service providers, management, or both.

Directors, managers, and superintendents are the people who shape the overall direction of organizations. They have great power both financially and politically. Although many early years collaboratives report that organizational leaders with positional authority participate in fewer collaborative opportunities than front-line service providers do, the impact of successful, collaborative relationships at higher levels has the potential to greatly shape the way families are served and supported in communities. Participation from both executive leaders and front-line staff is essential. How that may look will vary from community to community.

For example, consider a collection of small towns (numbering fewer than 10,000 people in total) located in a remote and isolated part of British Columbia. Their challenge was that front-line service providers worked together throughout the small communities but their employers lived and worked in larger centres far away from the area.

The local early years collaborative designed approaches to engage both groups: one approach for staff and one for management. This design, requiring structured communication and connections between the two groups, turned out to be an effective attempt to engage multiple levels within organizations. The result? An effort to increase integration and coordination among many organizations by affecting local programming operations as well as higher policy decisions.

Beware of choosing to engage policy makers alone. We have heard such comments from newly forming early years collaboratives as, "We don't want them if they aren't in a position to make decisions." We have also seen terms of references for groups that define and limit participation. It should be recognized that people bring multiple spheres of influence to a collaborative. If an election or choice process exists in your community, ask yourself:

- Who gets to make these kinds of decisions?
- How are other forms of influence valued?
- What is the difference in value between the ability to make a decision and the skill to help form a good decision?

Selection committees, limits on participation, and deference to power and privilege remind us too much of an episode of *Survivor*!

STUCK ON NUMBERS

When you view the *who* as a long-term and evolving process, you won't be concerned that not everybody is active and engaged all the time. Beware the common trap of getting stuck on the numbers. Countless meetings spend more time theorizing about why certain groups have not shown up than in honouring the folks who have. In early years community development, the players, both usual and non-traditional, will change. Work with anyone willing to help and keep the door open to new partners at any time.

"Whoever comes is the right people" is a principle promoted by Harrison Owen, co-founder of Open Space Technology. He has an original approach to gathering a diverse group to deal with complex issues in innovative and productive ways: He honours the voices that are present. Open Space Technology is a technique that explores the possibility of combining "the level of synergy and excitement present in a good coffee break with the substantive activity and results characteristic of a good meeting" (Owen, 1997, p. 3). If you consider the strategy of building relationships in early years community development as a long-term, ongoing, evolving version of Open Space Technology, then this principle suggests that the *who* is an important factor but not the ultimate factor in success.

Accept a continuum of participation levels. There will be very active participants alongside those who will stay informed but participate only occasionally. Further along the continuum, some people are simply more aware of early childhood issues while others will remain unaware and uninterested.

The *numbers* of people at the table is not a success indicator on its own. It is the *quality* of the interactions that deserve your attention. Measuring the impact of collaborative action or seeing program and policy changes that improve opportunities for children have more depth and are more useful as evidence. The goal is neither to increase numbers nor make everyone as devoted as the preacher. It is accepting where people are on the continuum of engagement that allows the collaborative to best leverage both individual and collective efforts.

That said, the result of like-minded people working together in a conflict-free zone tends to be complacency. People who feel comfortable, safe, and secure may generate positive energy but are ever in danger of becoming a "selection committee": a group that makes assumptions about others' suitability and that limits participation to a narrow range of interests and skill sets.

Be sure to engage with people and organizations that will offer different ways of looking at issues. The idea is not to convince and convert those with opposing views but to learn and grow and develop a shared understanding of the complexity of the issues. This, in turn, will enrich any decisions and actions that may result.

Whoever comes *are* the right people, and whoever is missing will provide depth when included. Implementing an inclusive approach to the early years community development process includes seeking new perspectives and strengths along the way.

HOW DO YOU CONNECT
WITH THE WHO?

*"Relationships can make all the difference
between reaching your goals
and merely coming close . . . having all
the skills and insights in the world
means nothing if you can't connect."*
— PETER S. TEMES, *THE POWER OF PURPOSE*

In early years community development, gathering the *who* is necessary for collaborative, collective action. Collaboration among multiple stakeholders is more than cooperation, it is more than coordination, and it goes farther and deeper than networking. How you start and maintain those connections influences whether collaboration is achieved and what it looks like. It is important to remain flexible, creative, and open to the possibilities that new, different, and sometimes conflicting perspectives bring to the topic of healthy children and healthy communities.

Be *deliberate* in finding ways to connect with all the possible stakeholders. This requires flexibility, creativity, and most importantly *patience*. Use a variety of strategies. A simple invitation may work to get the usual suspects involved. More consideration will be required to engage non-traditional partners. Give the connections time, build trust, demonstrate credibility, and always keep a door *open*.

Be deliberate!

Be patient!

Be open!

In a rural Early Years Collaborative, there was one key community organization that never seemed to come to any meetings or participate. The pattern over a number of years was an initial display of enthusiasm, followed by staff and administrative changes in the organization, followed by no communication from them for a year or two.

Assuming that you understand the dynamics occurring in other people's organizations is not helpful. In this case, the collaborative got the impression that the meetings were not relevant to the organization. They also perceived that some of that organization's staff members felt that their issues were in the minority and may not have been heard by the larger group.

After years of what seemed to be fruitless attempts at meaningful engagement — giving the organization money to work on related projects, personally delivering resources that were typically distributed at meetings, going out for coffee, asking advice, and a host of other attempts to build bridges — the organization complimented the early childhood coalition in public as being well connected, inclusive, and competent. Slowly, very slowly, staff tested the waters, showing up at a couple of meetings. Eventually the majority of staff members began to attend, signed up for extra working groups, and became strong advocates for the collaborative in the community.

Could their engagement have been fast tracked? Probably not.

Did the early years collaborative do everything right? Probably not.

Did a deliberate, patient, and open approach work in the end, or at least for now? It certainly did because both the collaborative and the organization developed a level of trust that was necessary for them to work together.

THE VIRTUE OF PATIENCE

Picking up where we were last observing our social experts . . .

We might expect all four of the children to be enthralled by the idea of joining their individual structures to make a larger group castle, but we would be wrong.

Tanner is certainly committed to *his* idea of everyone working together to build a castle they can fit into. Smiling with busy determination and focus, he knocks the blocks from his own structure until they are scattered on the ground. He is not aware that his idea has not caught on with the others.

Grace, Brynn, and Morgan are quietly fixing Brynn's original fallen structure but not really combining their own pieces. Morgan and Brynn's piles of blocks are in close proximity; the boundary lines are slowly blurring as to which belongs to whom. Their two piles naturally become one.

Tanner is poised on the outside of the play. He is prepared to bring his blocks to the group but waits for a sign that things are proceeding to fit his idea of castle building. He pauses and observes what the girls are working on and then poses a question to the group: "How will we fit in there?"

The educator responds with a query, "Hmmm . . . How will we fit?"

Tanner suggests a door made out of an L-shaped red block.

"Sure, that sounds great," the educator says. "Where would you like to put it?"

Brynn, Morgan, and Grace are now watching this transaction between the educator and Tanner. As Tanner is securing a doorway with the large red block, the educator passes Brynn a yellow block, involving her in the process. She adds the block but stops there.

At this point Grace catches on to the new theme of a larger structure and excitedly marches to Tanner's pile to help herself to one block, then two. Grace's own structure is set back, alone and untouched for the moment.

Brynn and Morgan are observing this new development, looking to the educator for guidance about what they should do.

"Place a block here?" Morgan asks.

The educator encourages her with a nod.

Tanner tries to get the others to hear his idea and offers yet another suggestion. "How about we build a castle and it will go up to the sky?"

Grace looks from the educator to Tanner, to Brynn, and to Morgan, trying to figure out her place in all of this. Back and forth her head is moving, her mind spinning with possibilities.

The educator speaks some encouraging and guiding words. "Let's try," she says, placing a block down to start the foundation of the expanded group castle.

While Morgan and Brynn choose to play independently, Grace follows this action, eager to join in but not entirely sure what this structure is all about.

Sensing the need for further team interaction, the educator introduces a new idea that involves all four village builders simultaneously.

"Look at this! This tower you built is *so* tall. Is it taller than you?" she asks Morgan, who is sitting close to her but is not fully into the play.

Morgan confirms that it is.

Brynn is watching. Grace and Tanner continue building until the educator asks, "Is it taller than Tanner?"

Will Tanner be distracted from his castle building to compare the height of the castle and himself and others?

Ask yourself:

- Do any pieces of this observation speak to a deliberate, patient, and open approach to relationship building?

- Are there different levels of engagement in the scenario? If so, are they equal in importance?

- Does everyone have influence? If so, how?

GIVE 'EM WHAT THEY NEED

One way to enhance the process of building relationships is to anticipate the needs of those you want to connect with. Being a part of any
process, movement, or project requires sensing or understanding the
relevance of the collaborative. Relevance is the third essential village-
raising strategy. We will explore it in greater detail in parts 4 and 5, but
it is worth taking some time now to consider how to make a gathering
relevant to diverse individuals and organizations.

First, consider what participants could get from being engaged
in early years community development. How does this work benefit
them? Then take that and package it in the form of an opportunity:
something that could be given to them. Here are some of the techniques that have worked:

- Serve food.
- Use a group technique such as Open Space Technology to
  start a conversation and find out what participants are passionate about. They may be looking for a place to express their
  hopes and concerns.
- Plan a fun, positive event designed to provide an opportunity for individuals and organizations to share what they are
  all about. They may feel isolated in their roles and crave some
  connection.
- What goes around comes around. Participate with energy and
  enthusiasm in other people's projects and efforts. They may
  need help getting great ideas off the ground.
- Serve food.
- Gather and share early years community development information that could be useful to individuals and organizations. They may be looking for new perspectives and learning
  opportunities.
- Find a way to financially compensate commitment from those
  who are unable to participate any other way. They may be

restricted by tight budgets from participating in something broader than their current role.

• Oh yeah, and serve food!

WHAT NON-TRADITIONAL PARTNERS WANT

Non-traditional partners can be a little more challenging to engage than the usual suspects. Take the business community, for example. There seems to be a big divide between it and the social service sector, except when one side (guess which) needs money from the other.

There is a better way to connect direct and indirect players in early years community development, and that is to ask questions. Why would they play a role in child development? How would a business benefit from efforts that support young children?

After much reading and interviewing, we have identified two primary arguments that connect the business community with early childhood development:

• Children are an investment in the future.
• Children are good for business.

Early years community developers can find the key leverage points that will pique the interest of the business community, or municipal government, or any major employers for that matter.

THE TIPPING POINT FOR BUSINESS

Members of a large Early Years Collaborative looked around the table at one another and commented (for the hundredth time) that businesspeople weren't at the table.

"Why don't they see this as important? How can we get them to see the value in what we are doing?" one asked.

After much dialogue, reflection, and a dose of reality, the group decided that the business world was completely foreign to the service providers around the table. And they suspected that the world of early years was just as foreign to the business community. A decision for action grew out of the questions that emerged from this dialogue:

- How *is* child development connected to business?
- Why *should* business care about the issues of children?
- What is the business community already doing, in their own way, to support families?

A few members of the collaborative went to the executive director of the local Chamber of Commerce. Uncomprehending glances were exchanged as the group falteringly shared their thoughts with him. Their goal was to offer to host a workshop designed specifically for the business community. They believed that this workshop would convince them not only that early years were important, but also that focusing on the early years would actually fill some of their needs. However, none of these needs was yet clear to the collaborative.

The tipping point in the conversation came when one of the early years members correctly read the executive director's defensive expression and bluntly stated, "We are not asking you for money!"

Whereupon the executive director smiled, leaned back in his chair, and began to show more interest in what was being said.

A series of planning meetings emerged from that meeting, engaging the Chamber of Commerce and two prominent businesses alongside the early years collaborative. The goal was to develop an event together that touched on topics that were useful to business and aligned with the issues of children. The event was designed much like a business symposium that included workshops and networking. The workshops included human resources topics, family-friendly tourism business practices, mapping resources, and economic arguments to support the role of business in early childhood — all packaged in an event that was not foreign to the target business audience.

A number of legacies resulted from this event. One is a

> Child and Family Friendly Business Award, which is awarded
> by the Chamber of Commerce annually in conjunction with
> the early years collaborative. Another is joint participation
> in a number of different community celebrations. But the
> most important is that relationships have been established.
> The overall approach was deliberate, patient, and open and
> will have long-lasting benefits for all involved.

On a national and international stage, the Committee for Economic Development in the United States hosted a conference in 2008 that focused on the many benefits of early care and education and provided a model for business leaders to become engaged in early child development advocacy. Attending were business leaders, aid agency representatives, and policy advocates. Key organizations that spoke included Heinz, Royal Bank of Canada, LEGO, IBM, and the World Bank.

The thrust of the event was to generate support in growing early child development programs aimed at promoting a healthy citizenry and a vibrant economy.

This gathering was the result of a number of other events across the United States: partnerships in Mississippi with the Economic Council, in Wisconsin with the Buffet Early Childhood Fund, and in Kansas with the Great Plains Energy Service.

The truth is, early childhood and business *are* linked. One role of early childhood community developers is to connect the dots, all the way from local "mom and pop" businesses right up to the massive corporations that drive national economies.

WHAT MULTICULTURAL COMMUNITIES KNOW

Communities that are well defined by some sort of culture, faith, or ethnicity often seem impenetrable, well protected, and even isolated from mainstream society. There may be rules and traditions that "the outside" is ignorant about. Being on the outside presents an initial barrier to connection. Outside groups, being unsure of protocol, often exclude themselves, which results in missed opportunities to learn and grow from diversity. What it takes is a special kind of approach, one that is deliberate, patient, and open.

Communities have formal and informal leaders. A leader may be a preacher, elder, or official, a special sort of person who knows and keeps the pulse of the people. The trust they develop in multiple communities enables them to bridge those communities.

In his book *The Tipping Point* (2002), Malcolm Gladwell calls these people "connectors" and describes their ability to connect with many subcultures as the ability to cause word-of-mouth epidemics — which is precisely what you may be after. When you find out who these leaders are, treat them as the gatekeepers. The community members will not trust you until the gatekeepers accept you. Get to know them, share the passion and goals of the early years collaborative, and be ready to learn a lot about how some incredibly connected communities are villages in and of themselves.

The Center for Law and Social Policy estimates that one out of every five children in the US is the child of an immigrant. The Center emphasizes the importance of finding immigrant leaders to serve as bridges to communities (Matthews & Ewen, 2006).

A collaborative located in a vibrant and culturally diverse urban centre in Canada faced ongoing struggles to connect with immigrant families raising their children in isolation. Language, culture, fear, lack of transportation, and lack of awareness were common barriers to families with young children — barriers that prevented them from taking part in early years programs designed to decrease their isolation and increase their access to appropriate social services.

The immigrant families that succeeded in overcoming the barriers were rewarded with immense social benefits for themselves and rich developmental experiences for their children.

The collaborative decided to build on these successes. It launched a concerted effort to engage more broadly with these immigrant communities. They decided to invest in families that had connected to programs and whose children were now entering the school system. These parents were offered training and support to become parent ambassadors between those in their culture with very young children and the early years programs.

In essence, the collaborative created gatekeepers or "connectors" who had a foot in both the immigrant community and the service community. It took intense trust building and communication to make it happen.

Being a parent ambassador involved attending a variety of programs on how to ease the transition for newcomers, offering translation and interpretation when needed, and being a face that other immigrant families felt connected to. In return, these volunteers received useful job-skills training.

Mia says, "If I had known about [this service] when I arrived as a new immigrant, my life would be so different . . . As a parent ambassador, I found that I can help people to share information and settle down easily. Parent ambassadors are all volunteers for the community, so there was no hesitation for me to be [one]. I got so much help from them so I really wanted to return some of it. There are so many people who are really desperate to get some help because of . . . language barrier or lack of information."

Ashley, a fellow parent ambassador, adds that "as an immigrant, I know newcomers will face some difficult period of adjustment . . . So I put that experience to use to help others . . . in that situation by volunteering."

RECOGNITION OF ABORIGINAL CULTURE

In 2006, Success by 6, an early years initiative in British Colombia, developed an Aboriginal Strategy that identified four priority areas designed to engage the Aboriginal Communities in BC — culture, language, self-determination, and self-governance — in a manner that respected their distinct culture and tradition.

Given that approximately 30% of the population of the province is of aboriginal ancestry, it was recognized that a mainstream approach to culturally rich and diverse populations would be ineffective and downright disrespectful.

Success by 6 works directly with Aboriginal communities to enhance the lives of young Aboriginal children and their families.

To support the implementation of its strategy, it has dedicated $3 million over the past three years through its Aboriginal ECD funding stream to support Aboriginal-identified priorities. Over 80 Aboriginal projects are funded annually and include twenty-two Aboriginal Coordinator positions, cultural resource development, training, and access to programs for children and families.

Innovative approaches have emerged. They are exciting examples of how bridges can be intentionally built to connect with diverse populations. For example:

- The provincial initiative circulated a DVD that communicated the importance of early childhood development in images and language that specifically speak to chiefs, elders, and other community leaders. It was made available on YouTube to widen its reach, scope, and usability (youtube.com/results?search_query=successby6bc).
- They put together a Grandpa and Granny Kit, a fun, interactive tool based on the tradition of learning language and culture from elders. The kit uses adorable puppets and can be adapted to the nuances of many First Nations.
- One community designed a creative approach for helping Aboriginal students to complete their college certification in early childhood care and education.
- Festivals and workshops were developed to celebrate Aboriginal children and to communicate to non-Aboriginal people about the issues, concerns, and goals of their culturally distinct neighbours.

HOW TO CONNECT WITH FAMILIES

Another group that requires some thoughtful consideration — families — is at the centre of the village. This population has the most at stake, but that doesn't mean it's easy to engage them. Their diversity makes them difficult to categorize. Families come in all sizes and configurations and at various education and economic levels.

How can a group of early years community developers be responsive to a parental perspective that is inclusive of the diversity that exists among families? There is no perfect answer. It is, however, important to give families the opportunity to share their thoughts in ways that fit their lives.

Have conversations — perhaps using the following case study as a starting point — to unearth perspectives on how to connect with families. Just as with all the other *who*s, be deliberate, patient, and open in developing a process to listen to and learn from families.

AN OPEN DOOR TO FAMILIES

A local Early Years Collaborative is working on their strategic plan. It addresses a variety of family-focused social, health, and education issues in the community. The group has agreed that families need to be involved in the process in some way. They are struggling with how to do that.

Anna suggests that local families should be invited to attend meetings. She proposes using the media to invite families to the meetings. She says that by having an open door, the collaborative will help parents feel that they have a place to direct their ideas and voice their needs.

Bob suggests that most of the people on the Early Years Collaborative are parents themselves — some with children under six. Could the group members just be the voice of parents as well as their organizations?

Chris feels that a couple of parents who frequently help out in her program would not be overwhelmed by the meetings and would love to attend and provide a parent perspective. The problem with this idea, she admits, is that these two parents are from a higher socio-economic bracket and won't necessarily be able to represent or speak for other families, for instance those who live in poverty.

Deborah admits that she did not feel her ability to contribute as a parent was as highly regarded when she was off on maternity leave and attended the collaborative as when she was tied to an organization. She believes that, in order to have meaningful growth, ownership of change and action must happen at the community level — in this case with families as the experts in their own destinies. She believes everyone has individual skills and perspectives to offer. Deborah asks the group, "So how can we respectfully include a family voice while recognizing that they cannot represent parents as a whole?"

Eli feels that the meetings are too complex for families. He feels that families would not work well in a strategic-planning meeting. He cautions the group about the danger of not being able to directly resolve parent concerns that are beyond the group's scope.

"Parents don't really have a voice at the table," he says. "It wouldn't be fair to them to involve them."

Freyja wonders if parents could be surveyed. Telephone surveys are good in terms of connecting with parents with limited literacy skills, she says. Paper surveys are another relatively inexpensive option. She offers to blanket the community with copies.

Glenda offers a suggestion that the group decides to learn more about: focus groups. Focus groups are a way for the Early Years Collaborative to interact directly with parents to ask for input.

Harvey reminds the group about a recent parent who contacted the collaborative with some programming concerns. He wonders how best to encourage other parents to feel free to voice their concerns and become involved.

In the end, this collaborative decides to get more

information by connecting with other communities to learn what has worked for them. One such effort brings them to a town similar in size that has a group that is parent-founded and parent-led and that serves as that collaborative's parent connection.

This parent group conducts community-wide parent surveys, participates in community meetings, compiles an e-mail distribution list to contact local families about events, presents parent perspectives about early childhood concerns to stakeholders, and writes letters of support for various funding opportunities.

In addition, they have developed an event schedule on Facebook intended to increase access of information to Internet-savvy families. Parents are encouraged to voice concerns to the collaborative, and in turn are incredibly valued for their involvement and input, bringing a more significant parent voice to the collaborative's process.

There are pros and cons to every idea. As the example above shows, the process of discovering the choices best suited to a community is important in building authentic, respectful relationships with families.

After you figure out how you are going to connect with families, figure out what you hope to learn from them. Here are some examples of questions that have been used by early years collaboratives to help them understand the experiences of parents and families. (Adapted from Make Children First Kamloops, 2009; Alberni Valley Make Children First Network, 2009.)

- What are the experiences of families raising young children in (your community)?
- What makes (your community) a good place to raise young children?
- Looking back, what community supports might have made a difference to you if they had been available?

- What resources, supports, or services do you find most valuable in your role as a parent? What may have prevented you from accessing any of these services?
- In what ways do families with young children perceive (your community) to be a child and family friendly city?

As the world continues to change, so, too, have the ways in which parents are supported in their roles.

In his book *Restoring Power to Parents and Places*, Richard Kordesh (2006) argues that parents may actually be receiving too much support. Our highly serviced and professionalized society, he says, has crowded parents out of their relationship with their children. Although organizations know that parent involvement is key to the success of any children's program, both non-profit mandates and entrepreneurs have horned into some of the roles that parents once held.

Kordesh argues that while it does take a village to raise a child, it will not happen without significantly greater contributions from productive families themselves. This perspective challenges efforts and mandates of organizations and governments. It leads communities to ask: Is there a best mix of services or do different families need a range of services to choose from?

Some people question the role of larger political and social bodies (such as governments, welfare institutions, health authorities, and education systems) in addressing the needs of children and families. They see government as a partner to, not a substitute for, adult leadership, good citizenship, and a caring village.

Yes, it's true that families are the foundation for children's experiences. But families thrive only with support.

Support is an ambiguous term, precisely because it looks different to everyone and can be found in different contexts. There are many kinds of support that a family may desire, need, or receive. They range from having a grandparent come over to play with the children while the parent goes grocery shopping to parental support groups for social connections. Yet another family feels strong and supported because of the valuable postpartum counselling and medical support they receive.

A balance needs to be found between the role of parents and the rest of the village, with the latter supporting parents not by *taking over* responsibility but by *freeing* them to love, nurture, and guide their children. The attunement of parent to child needs to be complemented by the attunement of community to family.

MOVING BEYOND THE WHO

There is no avoiding the fact that the *who* of early years community development is — and should be — complex and ever evolving. If it were not, the planning and work being done may not be relevant to the broad list of stakeholders who truly do have influence on healthy children and healthy communities. Does a nice, tidy, and tight community early years collaborative have the perspective and power to make long-lasting improvements? It might, but the glory of multiple perspectives is the big, complicated, energetic mass of relationships that is created. This creation can be far-reaching, especially when a structure is used to harness and direct the energy that has been sparked.

Let's suppose that you have brainstormed and discussed at length the *who* in your collaborative, resulting in a Hollywood "A" List of early years community development. You look around the table and see some usual suspects and some non-traditional partners. You see diversity and inclusion, a range of perspectives, strengths, and skills. This should work, right? Some organic magic should emanate from the connections between these people that will guide the collaborative into a peaceful path of networking bliss.

If only it were like that!

A synergistic magic does transpire when people interact and communicate, directly influencing momentum and commitment to action. The reality is that collaborative work will bring an array of dynamics, challenges, and complexity to the mix, requiring thoughtful and meaningful consideration and care. It's not enough just to have the "right players" around the table. Yes, you can count on relationships holding an energy that provides richness and exciting possibilities to raise the village. However, it's what we do with the relationships and the energy that matters and makes a difference.

ACTIVITY #4

BUILDING CONNECTIONS

General Idea

Building blocks are fun, a great way to remember the child within and a perfect tool to experience relationship building and the benefits of community collaboration. Ask a local child-care facility to share some small toy blocks.

What's Worked for Us . . .

STEP 1

Have people sit at tables in small groups.

STEP 2

Provide each person with at least five blocks.

STEP 3

Ask individuals to build a little tower with their blocks.

STEP 4

Relate this activity to services and programs for children.

Discuss this question: If organizations all do their own thing, creating their own little towers, how can families successfully navigate to find what they want and need?

STEP 5

Ask the small groups to build one group tower.

You can add extra challenges such as incorporating items other than blocks or holding a playful contest to build the most unusual or creative tower.

STEP 6
When the towers are finished (or your time is up) ask the large group what they noticed throughout the small group activity.
Answers may include: a change of energy, more enthusiasm, fun, a feeling of synergy, people connecting, and improved towers because there were more blocks to work with. Relate the activity back to the concept of the benefits of collaboration.

ACTIVITY #5

MAPPING THE WHO

General Idea
Explore the many potential relationships for an early years collaborative by mapping out and identifying *who* is in the community that can support or become involved with the early years.

What's Worked for Us . . .
STEP 1
Draw a relationship map.
Divide into small groups. Have every person in each group take a piece of paper and draw their collaborative in the centre (as a box, circle, or any shape they choose). Have the groups come up with as many organizations, partners, and relationships they can think of. Have them write/draw everything that comes to mind. Have them think of everyone who does, or could, or should play a part in early years community development. Who are the established partners, external supports, and natural allies? This map can be as creative or detailed as the groups desire.

STEP 2
Ask the small groups to pause, look at the map, and imagine the resources and strengths of the networking, learning and sharing that can occur when this many people/organizations work together. This is a collective look at community possibilities and another way of knowing and identifying your community.

STEP 3

Have each person in the small groups find their organizations on the map. Then individually draw a line that connects them to three relationships they already have. (Have them mark up the papers — they can draw roads or expressways!)

STEP 4

Each person is then challenged to identify and draw a circle around *one* connection that they would like to focus on and build on further (either a new one to build or an existing one to strengthen). Then, get them into pairs with these maps and share ways in which these relationships can be built. Each person should ask the other what has worked for them in their communities. Think of this map as a personal plan or commitment to go forth and build.

ACTIVITY #6

CHILDREN'S VOICES THROUGH ART

General Idea

Creating and enjoying art reminds us of what is important. This activity is a way to include the presence and voices of children in collaborative work that is typically full of adults.

What's worked for us . . .

STEP 1

Before the meeting, ask a child-care facility, preschool, and/or kindergarten to create some artwork following a theme you want to explore in the collaborative.

Some examples include:

What is community?

Who is in your village?

Every child has a right to . . .

What children need to feel loved is . . .

STEP 2

During the meeting, distribute samples of the art to small groups.

STEP 3

Ask groups to make notes of their reactions and discussions as they interpret the art.

STEP 4

Share discoveries with the larger group.

• *Variation:* Before receiving the artwork from children, ask collaborative participants to draw something related to the same topic. Analyse the sets together to celebrate both perspectives and see if this clarifies how adult thinking is aligned with or differs from that of children.

• *Variation:* Ask the participants to illustrate the topic themselves after their examination of the children's art. This will help people to integrate what they believe about the topic with what they have learned from the children.

• *Variation:* Provide a selection of families with young children with disposable cameras. Ask the children to take pictures of things related to your chosen topic. Encourage parents to have a dialogue with the children and decide on the picture composition together. Bring these photos to a meeting instead of the artwork.

PART 3
FRAMING LEADERSHIP

GOVERNANCE OF LEADERSHIP

"You will never be able
to hit a target you cannot see."
— Robin Sharma, *The Monk Who Sold His Ferrari*

Consider what happens when you build a house. Before you can get started, you need a design and a set of blueprints. The design is the general idea of what you are aiming for. The blueprints capture the steps and processes along the way. Some of these are big (the plumbing has to be installed before the drywall) and some minute (the windows must be installed 2.7 feet from the floor).

A friend of ours is currently building her home. We know that she has both written and unwritten agreements that help her manage this complex project. She has contracts with roofing companies and policies with insurance companies. She has also developed some informal and unwritten (and arguably just as important) processes with her husband: how they pick out the colour of the trim, how they choose bathroom fixtures that don't blow the budget, and how they will reach compromise when they want different things.

All these relationships require some structure to manage them, nurture them, and keep them alive and vibrant. Similarly, in early years community development you will find complexities created by personalities, personal agendas, organizational history, and conflicting perspectives that benefit from formal and informal structures.

Visualize the image of a village working together. What would happen if no assigned roles, responsibilities, duties, and/or systems or structures were in place? What if there were no defining parameters or boundaries of any kind? The result would likely be a state of anarchy, or the village itself might fold or collapse, unable to thrive or function. There is a reason that "society" functions with guidance and infrastructures, be they systemic, political, or social. Similarly, collaboratives also require structure. When it comes to raising a village, this structure comes in the form of governance: the governance of leadership.

WHAT GOVERNANCE OF LEADERSHIP MEANS

Governance of leadership . . . beep . . . beep . . . beep . . . We hear the plain language alarm going off. What is governance? It sounds so formal or political. What does it mean and what does it have to do with leadership or relationships?

Simply put, governance is the structure of how people relate to one another within the collaborative. By being intentional in articulating what collaboration looks like, it helps a collaborative move forward in a direction that maintains accountability. Consider it your file folder of blueprints or village guidelines for collective action, evaluation, and progress. Governance of leadership is also *how* relationships are built — where leadership and relationships meet.

In a group setting have you ever:
- felt unsafe to voice your opinion?
- felt unheard?

- been unsure of what is expected of you?
- wondered where you fit in?
- been unclear about other members' roles?
- been unsure how to bring information back to your organization?
- felt there was no process in place?
- thought the process was not inclusive . . . that not all of the *who* was part of the deliberation?
- wondered whether the group was on track?

If so, then governance is for you.

Governance describes the details of how the collaborative functions. The types and amount of detail will vary depending on the group's requirements and desires. Governance clarifies processes such as how a collaborative chooses to make decisions and how they choose to communicate with one another. Do they have a steering group and subcommittees, or do they make decisions on a Monday at noon while eating pizza on one leg?

Governance also helps individual participants see how they fit into the larger picture. Furthermore, articulating these structures helps communicate to others in the community how the collaborative works: that it is transparent and welcomes new perspectives.

To summarize, governance of leadership provides guidelines that clearly define how the members of a collaborative will relate to one another, how complexity will be handled, and how to move forward. It is a co-created and agreed-on definition of roles, responsibilities, reporting methods, leadership, and staffing as well as a collection of other possible dynamics.

A GOVERNANCE CHECKLIST

- Decision-making processes (consensus? voting? both?)
- Conflict-resolution strategies
- Chain of communication

- Vision, mission, guiding principles
- Celebrating group "norms" or culture
- How the work will get done
- How reporting will happen
- Responsibilities and roles
- Representation or membership (the who)
- The variety of methods used to create an open, free-flowing environment (techniques used, etc.)
- How evaluation will be used and who is accountable to the evaluation findings.

In *Social Intelligence*, Daniel Goleman describes the necessity of structured processes in working together. "If we are to shift to more humane organizations, change will be required at two levels: within the hearts and minds of those who provide care and in the ground rules — both explicit and hidden — of the institution" (Goleman, 2006, p. 253).

HOW, WHY, AND WHEN

While the term "governance" sounds on the formal and rigid side, the best approach is to attain a balance of formality and informality that best suits the group and that evolves as the group develops. Formally, governance takes the shape of a framework of written documents. Informally, governance is the culture and spirit of working together.

What do people need to feel comfortable, connected, and willing to contribute? Getting this balance is important because details of a collaborative's structure may help some and scare others away. They may increase safety for some and limit participation for others.

Picture a collaborative that has worked together successfully for over ten years. They have learned to balance action, change, and relationship dynamics, including conflict. You would think that this group has a detailed governance structure in place to guide them through ten years together, right? Think again. All of this was done *without* a formal governance structure. Instead, the collaborative had an unspoken, informal, yet viable governance structure.

That said, ten years on, this collaborative began to explore more formalized structures.

Why now? For this group, the longer they worked together, the more complex the issues became. They spent the first years getting on the same page to promote early childhood messages and better understand local issues. The result was action and community mobilization, with the group becoming a model for other communities.

With growing success, both locally and as a model, the group began to experience a change in their membership. Many new members came and went over the course of a year. Articulating to the new members what the collaborative is and *how* they operated together became essential to sustaining the new membership. For example, one woman wrote this on her meeting evaluation: "I felt like I was entering a ten-act play at act six. I felt lost." A governance structure would help orient this new member.

Although the lack of a governance structure initally helped the group to grow and thrive, ten years later it was making it difficult for new members to create meaningful connections.

Other early years community development collaboratives integrate governance into their structure at the beginning stages of development. For example, another early years group launched itself by creating formal terms of reference and committee and subcommittee structures, objectives, and procedures. It worked for them largely because of the size of their community. Urban settings usually involve the dynamics of size, more "territory" to guard, and more people who are unfamiliar with each other.

In the case of this collaborative, formal structures were helpful at the beginning because the community needed formal evidence of safety and trust to begin working together. As the collaborative grows, however, it will be important for members to be mindful of how (and when) flexibility may encourage enhanced community connections.

Drawing from their experiences, authors Donna McLeod and Varina Russell write, "It is common for collaboratives, during challenging times, to call for more policies, procedures, and guidelines and then, in short order, find those same policies and procedures stifling for the new task at hand. Broad guidelines can have more staying power than highly detailed procedures. Detailed procedures, however, can be very useful for targeting purposes, particularly if there is no expectation that they will automatically generalize to other situations" (McLeod & Russell, 2007, Module Six.). Flexibility within governance of leadership may look like a broad, even vague infrastructure that allows evolution to occur.

What happens to relationships when governance is rigid and imposed? Sometimes a cookie-cutter approach to collaboration is dropped into a community, often with the best intentions. As a result, however, the development of shared meaning is diminished, which leads to a lack of ownership and a sense of disconnection. When governance is not defined and managed by the group itself, the group no longer does community development work, becoming an agenda-driven project instead.

There is no right or wrong time to explore the evolution of governance of leadership. Nor is there one magic formula for what should be included in your governance structure — including, for that matter, what you want to call it.

As will become clear in the next two chapters, governance is supported by two other leadership activities: facilitative leadership and shared leadership. How these are utilized will greatly affect a collaborative's governance.

FACILITATIVE LEADERSHIP

Leadership is an unwieldy topic. Even reflecting upon our favourite leadership quotes from chapter 2, the field of study is wide. The next two chapters of this book carve off a little piece of leadership as it applies directly to supporting an early years collaborative: facilitative leadership and shared leadership.

To get a picture of the former, envision family puzzle night. Parents and children are huddled around the kitchen table, each person focused on their favourite section. The group activity looks suspiciously like loosely connected, almost isolated individual action. Often, one member of the family will claim the edge pieces while others will be drawn to single sections of the picture. With luck, someone will take on the role of facilitative leader. This person keeps the bigger project in mind, reminding the rest of the family to join their sections. Such a person tends to have an eye for finding the connecting pieces in order to bring the whole puzzle together.

The facilitative leadership function is exactly what is needed in early years community development. Community work is typically not in most people's job descriptions. It is generally done off the side of their desks and often only because of the person's passion and interest. Although many people see the potential in big-picture planning, networking, and ultimately collaboration, most don't have time to spare for a community process that may not have direct and immediate benefits to their job or clients. Some make the time only to discover that committees and meetings degenerate into an unending rhythm of talking and planning because no one ever has that extra time for the "doing" part. The opposite imbalance can occur as well. Reactive, knee-jerk action can result in the exclusion of key voices and a departure from an overarching goal.

The secret, of course, is to find a balance between process and action.

Building a collaborative is a craft that requires the facilitative leadership of a dedicated person (or people). Although the position is often designated as manager or coordinator, this role could also be called facilitator, catalyst, convener, change agent, or leadership developer. Having a dedicated facilitative position for moving the work and voices of a collaborative forward is one way to make room on the desks of those who don't have the time, energy, permission, or passion to do so.

Facilitative leadership is about maximizing opportunities for an early years collaborative. Here's how David Chrislip describes facilitative leadership positions: "They help create and support an inclusive and constructive process, convince others that collaboration is necessary, help do the initiating work, convene the stakeholders, keep them focused and engaged, and link stakeholders with formal decision-making bodies and implementing organizations. Their capacity to accomplish these tasks depends on their credibility" (Chrislip, 2002, p. 88).

Sometimes, collaboratives have revolving chairs instead of a dedicated facilitative leader or team. These are people who step into the role of change agent on a rotating basis. Dedicated facilitation, however it is structured, ensures that the collaborative process is guided by someone neutral. This is key because members who are representing an organization are in danger of being territorial about their programs and institutional interests.

Neutrality can be interpreted in different ways. At a community dialogue session we attended, consultants Ali Grant and Margaret Steele (2009) asked the participants whether neutrality could be seen as "someone who acts from a level of care and concern for *all of us*, rather than care and concern *for me*, or care and concern for *people like me?*"

The neutral facilitator is someone who can unite and blend and work through many competing agendas to get to the core of the collaborative's mission. Someone who can pull a variety of perspectives together into a beautiful kaleidoscope as opposed to reflecting on the colouring of their particular organization's perspective and mandate.

STRONG SCAFFOLDING

Picture a heritage site, cathedral, castle, or even a modern glass-covered skyscraper. When workers restore brick, paint walls, or wash windows, what do they do first? They cover these structures with scaffolding, a temporary structure made up of an assortment of poles and platforms. The scaffolding has a strong and sturdy foundation but can easily be disassembled and moved to a new location that requires work.

Early childhood educators are familiar with the concept of scaffolding in a different context. It was a term based on the work of Lev Vygotsky, which gained popularity in the late 1970s to describe an effective way to give children the support they need during learning opportunities. This was evident in the interactions between Tanner, Morgan, Grace, and Brynn and the early childhood educator. Think about this in the case of this educator.

- She came prepared. Having checked the ages of the children beforehand, she packed an abundance of age-appropriate materials and inquired about the play space in order to anticipate any needs, safety concerns, or distractions.
- She asked: "Shall we build together?" This type of comment acted as a prompt or suggestion to get the play started but also encouraged the children to consider the possibility of working together.
- She asked open-ended questions. She tried many different techniques to engage the children in play and followed their lead by demonstrating an inclusive, flexible approach.
- She consistently acknowledged the group's efforts, prompting the children to reflect on their actions.

An extension of the scaffolding analogy can be applied to collaboratives and how an early years community development leader facilitates and supports them. This person may be paid, or may volunteer, perhaps squeezing activities into breaks from their regular job. Regardless of who they are, they act as artists, craftsmen, visionaries, and mediators in their role of scaffolding and supporting the work of the collaborative.

Vygotsky suggested that children are capable of greater learning success when they have flexible assistance from adults (or other children) in a joint learning process (Gonzalez-Mena, 2009). Early childhood educators scaffold children's learning by structuring their environments, modelling and celebrating play for them, and introducing them to new opportunities. Similarly, we suggest that early years collaboratives are capable of greater collaboration when they have flexible leadership that structures environments, models collaboration, and introduces the membership and beyond to future possibilities.

FACILITATIVE LEADERSHIP ROLES

- MEETING PLANNER: Considers planning agendas and process, goes over previous minutes, prepares for the meeting, makes sure that refreshments will be provided, reviews space and location ahead of time.

- MEMBERSHIP RECRUITER: Is vigilant about issues of recruitment, orientation, ongoing contact, support, and encouragement.

- COORDINATOR: Facilitates special events and projects, prioritizes the day to day work based on the collaborative's direction, and is accountable for the finances of the collaborative.

- FACILITATOR: Is careful to be objective, inclusive, proactive, and flexible, always engaging multiple learning styles.

- RELATIONSHIP MANAGER: Employs conflict mediation, builds trust, pulls out all voices, and cheerleads.

- VISION KEEPER: Stimulates big-picture thinking, strategic planning, and the connections that promote possibilities.

- RESEARCHER: Performs the tasks of data collection, process and outcome evaluation, and collection of information required between meetings.

- INFORMATION CONDUIT: Shares the latest academic research, connects organizations to funding sources, and promotes professional development opportunities that benefit collaborative participants.

- AGENT OF CHANGE: Supports the advocacy of social policy change, general importance of the early years, and engages in social marketing efforts aimed at both public and political audiences.

How does a community unearth such a person?

First, one person doesn't have to embody every item in that list. Like superheroes, a super-facilitator isn't likely to exist. A combination of qualities that best match the needs and characteristics of the collaborative is what we're talking about.

Second, it may be possible to create small teams to increase overall leadership capacity.

Third, what we are describing (especially in terms of issues related to children) is a profession that doesn't formally exist. It's not quite a general facilitator, it's not quite a community economic-development expert, it's not an expert in child development, and it's not quite a project manager or executive director. It's none of those things and all of these things. We call ourselves Early Years Community Developers.

One goal of facilitative leadership is to build a capacity for collaboration in everyone. Think back to the family puzzle night and the role of the facilitative leader: someone who keeps the bigger project in mind, reminding the rest of the family to join their sections together. He or she acts as a connector and aims to raise the profile of early years community development work.

The goal of Early Years Community Developers is to get organizations to increasingly include community work as an essential component in their organizational culture. When organizations reflect community collaboration in their mandates, mission statements, and job descriptions, they signal to their staff that community work is valued and participation is supported.

The way to move toward collaboration is to "move the scaffolding around." Facilitative leadership enables shared leadership to emerge.

SHARED LEADERSHIP

"Leadership is not the private reserve of a few charis-
matic men and women. It is a process
ordinary people use when they are bringing forth
the best from themselves and others."
— KOUZES AND POSNER, *THE LEADERSHIP CHALLENGE*

Now that we have emphasized the need for dedicated facilitative leadership, is it not contradictory to say that the second part of the leadership equation is *shared* leadership? Think of it this way: Dedicated leadership that is facilitative in nature actually promotes shared leadership.

The concept of shared leadership can be found in business, education, and even parenting literature. We came to our epiphany about how it fits with early years community development, however, when we took a break from research and writing to rent the movie *First Knight*, starring Sean Connery.

Although of course glamourized by Hollywood, the movie illustrates how King Arthur developed his relationships with the knights of the round table. It even showed the mythical round table engraved with the words: "In serving each other, we become free." It is the serving of one another — when everyone steps up to the table and contributes their "all" to shared leadership — that is truly collaborative.

David Perkins (2003) uses the tale of King Arthur as an analogy to describe power and leadership in collaborative conversations. He writes that with a round table there is no foot and no head. All who sit around it are equals. In the case of the knights of Camelot, that included the King himself.

As Perkins puts it, "The symbolism of place at the table is something we all feel, whether we're sitting in a boardroom, jury room, ready room, team room, or an ad hoc let's-solve-this-problem meeting in the corner of the corporate cafeteria. We may not be ready to challenge our colleagues to duels, but long tables . . . inevitably provoke uneasy thoughts about status" (Perkins, 2003, p. 2).

The greatest contribution a leader can make is to provide opportunities for others to develop and exercise leadership. This chapter contains three ideas to foster shared leadership:
- identify and draw forth leaders
- create a power balance among participants in a collaborative
- and keep adjusting and learning through evaluation and reflection.

WHO ARE THE LEADERS?

Review the following checklist and reflect personally on leadership within your early years collaborative. Who:
- acts as a catalyst, energizer, and facilitator?
- creates the vision?
- seeks out new partnerships and perspectives?
- makes sure that process includes action, and action is balanced with mindful process?

- is inspiring to others?
- does all the work?
- encourages participation?
- invests energy in relationship and trust building?
- reminds the group about different values, cultures, generations, and economic situations?
- embraces the learning from frustrations and conflict?
- works at sustaining the commitment to group process even through difficulties and distractions?

Shared leadership is carefully distributed leadership that enhances and utilizes the skills and knowledge of a group. It also holds individuals accountable for their contributions to the collective action and resulting outcomes.

So how do you make this happen? It certainly isn't always easy. Why? Because shared leadership isn't the way organizations typically operate and because of the territorial qualities that multiple groups bring to collaboratives.

THE LION'S DEN

TRACY

Sometimes our biggest lessons and most significant milestones are achieved when things need to change. In the very early days of our community collaborative, there was a sense of excitement and impatience to work more formally together. With the collaborative on the verge of evolving into a larger, stronger, and more influential group, some members perceived a power imbalance that they feared (and rightly so) would destroy the potential for authentic collaboration.

Money, power, and territory — the three monkeys on the back of group collaboration — reared their ugly heads. When our collaborative received financial recognition to formally fund the work of the table, many questions surfaced. Who held the purse strings? How much control did the collaborative actually have? How many representatives from one organization could tip the balance of power during meetings? Would one strong and well-funded sector be allowed to drown out the voices of others? Why was early child development only then being recognized as important when people had been working unacknowledged in the trenches of early childhood care and education for decades?

What started out as monkeys grew quickly to full-size gorillas. The early childhood care and education community called on me to face the fact that these concerns were valid and were a threat to the life course of our community early years collaborative unless they were addressed, and soon. In a meeting (which in retrospect I now describe as entering the lion's den), I went, listened, and really heard their major fear: that any shared ownership and true commitment within the collaborative was in jeopardy if there wasn't a significant effort to level the playing field and ensure that all voices were heard.

I emerged from the lion's den having learned my first of many lessons about leadership: where it is found and how to use it both in myself and in the people I work with.

Achieving shared leadership is one way to balance power and territory. This is the key point of the story, but if you are interested in knowing the result of our struggles, consider that:

- We began a very positive journey to build the capacity of the early childhood care and education sector in our community by showing how much we valued every voice. The collaborative designated funds to cover the costs of a substitute to ensure participation from the child-care field.
- In addition, we developed a budget subcommittee so financial direction was transparent and owned by the collaborative members.
- Finally, we emerged with deeper trust — in fact, we often refer to the lion's den as a time when assumptions were challenged, truths were spoken, and leadership began to be shared.

EVALUATION SUPPORTS LEADERSHIP

Leadership is strengthened when we can carve time out from our day-to-day busywork to reflect on the difference that the collaborative journey is making. There are different types of evaluations for weighing projects and events accomplished by the group and the process used in creating them. The best evaluative approach is not after the fact; it is one that considers, at the outset, what is important to learn and how that learning will be captured while remaining open to anything unexpected.

Evaluation provides an opportunity to listen to one another and to use what is heard in order to learn, evolve, and move forward together. However, people often don't know what to do with the information when they receive the results. They politely say, "Hmmm, that's interesting . . ." However, if they don't engage with it, the opportunity from the evaluation is wasted.

We offer you a challenge to make your evaluation more than just "interesting." After all, evaluations have the potential to be meaningful and useful while enhancing the shared leadership around the table.

Here are some ways of engaging in evaluation in order to support leadership:

- Take part in a community of practice: Share resources and experiences in order to evaluate your own practices.
- Join together online: Find a group that promotes community and leadership reflection (for example, Tamarack – An Institute for Community Engagement, tamarackcommunity.ca).
- Use meeting evaluations: Listen to one another, honour what is shared, and *use* evaluation responses in planning future direction and creating further dialogue.
- Connect with advisories: Seek other early years community developers at local, regional, provincial, or national levels who can assist in evaluating the big picture.

- Hold interviews: Ask various levels of partners how things are working from their perspective. Include funders, families, and the general community in this. Use this feedback to guide the work.
- Journal: Take time to reflect on the collaborative work and capture on paper things that work well and things to explore in the future.
- Hire an external evaluator: Take a break from the evaluative role and invite an outside perspective to observe.
- Review successes: Find out what works well for people and build on it. Celebrate!
- Revisit: Check back with the group about shared hopes and desired outcomes and examine what has changed and why.
- Ask: "How do we know when our work has an impact?"
- Reflect: "Do we practice shared leadership?"

Looking at the bigger picture of evaluation means asking whether the whole concept of building capacity to support healthy early child development is valid. How can we capture evidence that early years community development efforts are working? Do these efforts nurture the village so it can raise its children to have lives that are full, rich, rewarding, and productive?

One example of an evaluation system is the Community Capacity Building for Early Childhood Development in British Columbia. This groundbreaking evaluation and reporting system looks at how communities support the development of all children and families in the areas of community-driven planning and coordination, service delivery, and local awareness and mobilization. The system employs an online survey, which gives not only to community facilitators but also to *all* the people who make up the *who* (community stakeholders and partner organizations).

Community Action Reports are generated based on local conversations about successes and challenges. Analysed at a provincial level, the data are useful for the province as well as individual communities.

For more information, supporting documents, and the survey itself, explore the Success by 6 Website at http://www.successby6bc.ca/early-childhood-development/resources

This type of group self-evaluation enables collaboratives to adjust and learn about the process of working together. We have learned through the experience that not only does the process offer an opportunity to reflect on building community capacity, it also lays the pathway to foster shared leadership within the collaborative. It does so by helping facilitative leadership be accountable with the many stakeholders in the community and, together, implement action.

FROM BLUEPRINTS TO CONSTRUCTION

So now you have leadership guiding the collaborative and leadership leveraged within the collaborative. The outcome of these two things is a credible driving force ready to make changes that will improve the lives of children and families. Your approach makes a bigger impact because systemic changes affect things in communities, regions, provinces or states, countries, and (we hope) even globally.

This brings us back to the discussion of governance in leadership at the beginning of this section. Facilitative leadership and shared leadership require an evaluative and operational structure that allows everyone to have a role in thinking, planning, and doing.

Of course, in order to do so, individuals must find how the collaborative work is relevant to them.

ACTIVITY #7

LOOKING AT LEADERSHIP

General Idea

Leadership is a vast subject and one worth exploring in a collaborative. Increase awareness about personal leadership qualities by learning from materials, resources, and each other.

What's Worked for Us . . .

STEP 1

Decide as a group what kinds of leadership approaches you want to explore. Here is a list to get you started thinking. Some are historical and some are more contemporary.

Artful leadership	Autocratic leadership	Behavioural leadership
Charismatic leadership	Collaborative leadership	Community leadership
Creative leadership	Cross-cultural leadership	Democratic leadership
Emergent leadership	Emotional leadership	Entrepreneurship leadership
Facilitative leadership	Functional leadership	Laissez-faire leadership
Level 5 leadership	Meritocratic leadership	Organizational leadership
Participative leadership	People-orientated leadership	Quantum leadership
Quiet leadership	Relations-orientated leadership	Servant leadership

Shared leadership	Situational leadership	Spiritual leadership
Strategic leadership	Taoistic leadership	Task-orientated leadership
Transactional leadership	Transformational leadership	Visionary leadership

STEP 2

Have each person pick *one* leadership approach from the list and find a document on the topic, whether a book, an article, or a Web-based resource. Encourage people to take notes because they will return to the group and pass on what they have learned about that particular leadership style. What catches your attention?

STEP 3

After reading, break into groups of three. Each person shares the highlights of what they have learned from their solo reading time. Ask one another questions. Share the juicy leadership pieces that stand out.

STEP 4

Reflect on how you might use this learning within the collaborative.

• *Variation:* Begin to write a personal leadership statement (many resources are available on how to write such a statement). Use the leadership information shared in the group to find what resonates for individuals. There is not just one way to lead. Everyone possesses various leadership styles and will find that different styles fit different situations.

• *Variation:* Instead of a long list of leadership approaches, print out leadership quotes that capture a variety of qualities. Ask people to pick a quote that speaks to them and read it aloud. The quotations can then be posted on the wall as a constant reminder of the diverse leadership in the room.

ACTIVITY #8

SHOPPING SPREE — BY CONSENSUS

General Idea

Need to make some collaborative decisions? How about designating funds by consensus? This activity can be used to identify whole group priorities. This can be done as a practice, with fake funds, or for real, based on the collaborative's budget. The shopping spree process is structured to make each participant feel that they have contributed in the decision making.

What's Worked for Us . . .

STEP 1

Before the shopping spree is planned, have someone pull together possible shopping items. These may have come from previous dialogues, from an online survey, or from a current strategic plan. Attach a cost estimate to each idea.

STEP 2

Create a worksheet for each participant (see below).

STEP 3

As a large group, review the worksheet. Without getting into any discussion, clarify items. At this time, it is important to review what consensus means. Find a definition that makes sense for the group. Ours is:

Consensus involves collaboration, rather than compromise.

Work together to achieve a position when everyone in the group can say, "I can live with it."

This means that though all participants may not find the outcome an ideal solution, they acknowledge that it isn't worth arguing about. They can live with it, support it, and get to sleep at night.

STEP 4
Allow time for individuals to fill out their personal choices for funding allocation. No talking at this time!

STEP 5
Have participants form pairs. Their task is to review their individual lists and come to consensus on a new, co-created list. Negotiation, learning, and openness are required.

STEP 6
Join pairs together to form quads. Ask each quad to create one list by consensus.

STEP 7
Join quads into groups of eight and repeat. Keep adding groups together until you have two halves of the whole group.

STEP 8
Allow each of the two groups to present their shopping list.

STEP 9
As one large group, compare the final two shopping lists and note similarities and differences. Facilitate creatively until there is only one shopping list that everyone can live with.

SHOPPING SPREE						
List	Price Range (estimate)	Personal	Pairs	Quads	8's	Large Group
Example: Parent Focus Groups, media campaign, or workshop						
Total to Spend:						

ACTIVITY # 9

EVALUATION: RED, YELLOW, GREEN

General Idea

Look to the design of a traffic light to help groups evaluate any issue, topic, or project that they are working on as a collaborative. This activity gives the group a visual way to evaluate an issue by considering the many perspectives and the many sides. (A heartfelt thank-you to our creative colleague Brenda West for this one.)

What's Worked for Us . . .

STEP 1

Clearly describe an issue, topic, initiative, or project that is of interest to the group.

STEP 2

Place a stack of green, yellow, and red slips of paper or sticky notes on small tables. Take time for personal reflection. Ask individuals to sort any thoughts, feelings, facts, ideas, or reactions they have to the topic by writing on the colored paper.

> RED = Stop! Each person writes on the red paper any negative implications or concerns they see: things that make them hit the brake on this idea, issue, or project.

> YELLOW = Caution! Slow the process down. On the yellow paper, jot down any special considerations or required clarifications from a personal perspective.

GREEN = Go! The green paper is for any positive reactions: partnership potential, innovative additions, things that inspire or excite people about the project.

STEP 3

Post the individual coloured papers in a central spot. We used a piece of flip-chart paper designated with three "traffic light" circles. The red slips go onto the red circle, and so on. Avoid questioning people's reactions or opinions at this stage, and resist passing judgment on what has been expressed. This is simply a time for individuals to evaluate how they feel about an issue and learn how others are feeling. A large group dialogue to sort through these items (like finding common themes) can follow.

PART 4

CONSTRUCTING RELEVANCE

GROUNDING RELEVANCE

" . . . community development as a process . . .
somehow engages all who enter into action
as both givers and receivers."
— LEE J. CARY, EDITOR, COMMUNITY DEVELOPMENT AS A PROCESS

"What is the *relevance* of that question, your honour?" Flick through the television channels and chances are you will hear this statement booming from the mouth of an indignant lawyer on any number of popular judicial or legal shows. Often the actor, portraying an incensed legal representative, is appealing to a judge to see the weakness in the opposing party's argument.

In contrast to the argumentative nature of the courtroom, the concept of relevance can also be applied to look for the positive meaning, clarity, and connection between each participant and the early years collaborative. Grounding relevance encourages people to look closely — to really stop and reflect — on their involvement in a collaborative. Thinking and talking about relevance will reveal the connections that exist for participants. Exploring both individual and organizational relevance helps us learn why people come, why they stay, and what keeps the momentum going over the long term.

Relevance starts with the individual person making some kind of connection with a collaborative effort. A Give/Get conversation, for example, can reveal for a person a greater awareness of their personal motivation, hopes, and purpose in being part of a collaborative. There is no single right or wrong reason for being involved.

For a connection to occur for an individual, it must occur in their own brain. In other words, the connection must take place in a way that makes sense to them. The stronger the connection a person sees between themselves and the work, the more enthusiasm and energy they will feel they are able to devote. Create a space for personal reflection and ask the question: What do you give and what do you get from an early years collaborative?

Instead of being just another mandated or disengaged meeting, a collaborative meeting takes on greater meaning and purpose when you explore how it relates to and taps into the passion of each member. Grounding relevance looks at the connections between *your thinking* and *your actions*.

How do you draw out these connections? Our simplified answer is to develop a place and practice of personal reflection. By reflection we mean giving individuals time to sit with perceptions and thoughts and then encouraging ways to expand their thinking. As Henry Mintzberg writes, "Reflecting does not mean musing, and it is not casual. It means wondering, probing, analyzing, synthesizing, connecting" (Mintzberg, 2004, p. 254).

When people *see* how they fit into the bigger picture of what the collaborative is doing *and* how well it enhances their organizational or personal philosophies, something interesting happens: They find what they can contribute and commit to.

For example, a kindergarten teacher shared that participating with an early years community collaborative has renewed her as an educator.

Her career has been dedicated to quality learning experiences in the classroom with a strong emphasis on play. A teacher's job is often isolated from things that are going on in the community because her focus is on the time when she is engaged with her class. As part of an effort to build bridges between the early childhood community and the school district, the local early years collaborative began to pay the costs of a substitute teacher so a kindergarten teacher could attend daytime meetings. After several years, the local school district saw the benefits of this participation and assumed the costs.

Professionally, the teacher began to learn more about the services and people working with children before they entered the school system. Her ongoing participation in collaborative planning helped her meet the needs of children transitioning into kindergarten classrooms. She has since had the opportunity to share, at a national event, her commitment to grassroots community development and her belief that it is critical for schools to work together with other early childhood services in order to offer a holistic and consistent support to families.

In this situation, the kindergarten teacher renews her passion and validation. In turn, she gives back by sharing both her perspective as a teacher at the collaborative meetings and the collaborative experience at the kindergarten teachers' meetings.

REFLECTION STARTERS FOR A GIVE/GET DIALOGUE

We have developed a Relevance Survey to help individuals and their respective organizations learn what they got out of being part of our early years collaborative. The survey included these questions:

1. How long have you been a participant in the collaborative?

2. If you left your organization, to what extent do you think it would maintain its involvement with the collaborative?
    Not at all
    A little bit
    A fair amount

3. Choose what your organization gives or gets from the following resources as a result of its involvement with the collaborative:
    effective networking
    leadership
    relevant communication
    client referrals
    the ability to leverage outside resources, recognition, organizational strengths and skills, and information

4. To what extent does the collaborative influence your organization to make new or altered programming decisions?
    Not at all
    A little bit
    A fair amount

5. To what extent are you personally connected with these aspects of the work (answer with *not at all, a fair amount,* or *to a great extent*):
    vision
    goals
    projects
    meetings
    subcommittee work

6. Choose what you personally give or get of the following from the Network:
    bigger reach into community
    recognition
    personal satisfaction
    effective networking

knowledge/skill development
leadership
and/or other

7. How clear is your role and responsibility as a
collaborative participant?
    Not at all
    A little bit
    A fair amount

8. To what extent do we, as a collaborative, recognize and
fully utilize the strengths and skills of each participant?
    Not at all
    A little bit
    A fair amount

9. Assess the sense of community within the Collaborative
based on your experience of the following (answer with
not at all, a fair amount, or *to a great extent*):
    Your opinions are heard and respected
    You have opportunity for informal networking/social
    activities
    You trust the collective
    You feel you are an integral part of both process and
    outcome
    You share responsibilities
    You share the group vision

The most notable results of this survey include the sense that
people felt they got more than they gave both organization-
ally and personally. At the same time, not one respondent
indicated that there was *not* a sense of community. The area
with the greatest growth potential was "shared responsibility" — which, interestingly, is tied to giving.

The overall survey responses allowed the collaborative to realize
that engaging and retaining people is complex and ever-changing, as

is seeing the connection. The questions gave each participant time to reflect and to renew their commitment by taking a closer look at why they were involved in the collaborative work, as well as at what helps them stay and what helps boost relevance.

In their book *Great Connections: Small Talk and Networking for Business People*, Anne Barber and Lynn Waymon reveal how to use small talk and give/get discussions to make great connections. "Any relationship is created and solidified if you and your partner exchange something — an experience, an idea, a phone number . . ." (Barber & Waymon, 1992, p. 25). The idea of sharing an experience with another person encourages a look at the benefits of collaborative involvement beyond our own immediate gains. It becomes less about what we can *get* and more about what we can *give* and how we can learn and connect with others.

LEARNING ABOUT "US"

One way connections happen is through well-crafted introductions and activities — times when a meeting steps lightly into personal topics.

When collaborative participants have the opportunity to learn about one another outside of work, the interpersonal connections become more relevant. People feel good when they are able to share things such as family traditions, their favourite children's book, or how they are feeling at that moment.

You don't have to devote the entire meeting to such explorations but can, instead, encourage brief but meaningful glimpses into what makes us who we are, and what connects us to each other and the early years group. Other things to share include:

- favourite children's songs and rhymes
- the location of your early childhood home
- the names of your grandparents or ancestors — your family origins
- your organization's mission and elevator speech

- the number of children and families you serve
- exciting initiatives going on in your organization
- ideas for reducing stress
- words associated with "parenting"
- seasonal traditions
- your definition of "play"
- something new inspired by a new baby
- highlights from the past year.

Sharing this type of personal information brings about togetherness. Building on personal relevance can help us look at ways to expand our thinking and experience a collective relevance.

CONSTRUCTING
COLLECTIVE RELEVANCE

*"Civilization is the process in which
one gradually increases the number of people
included in the terms 'we' or 'us' and at the
same time decreases those labeled 'you' or 'them'
until that category has no one left in it."*
— HOWARD WINTERS, QUOTED BY A. CANTWELL IN
HOWARD DALTON WINTERS: IN MEMORIAM

Shared vision . . . shared values . . . common ground . . . commit-ment . . . shared stake . . .

As we worked to capture and describe what happens when an early years collaborative really clicks, we tried applying all of the above terms. While all of them need to be present in a group, something was missing. We struggled to find words for the magic that emerges when groups get to the heart of working together.

Collective Relevance (CR) is the term we came up with after many, many hours of conversations about the something more, the *magic* that shows up in a brand new way of thinking and is translated into benefits for both the individuals and the collaborative as a whole.

Wow, this sounds earth shattering! It is, and isn't. Having experienced CR, it does feel special, even powerful, *and* seems to hold transformational qualities. At the same time, there is no drum roll, no fancy lady jumping out of a cake, and no voiceover saying, "What a feeling of CR today!" Being drawn to the feeling, however, we have researched, reflected, and experimented with describing CR as well as finding practical ways to experience it and sustain it.

CR is seeing the whole. It is a way of feeling, creating, and thinking together. It is what a group can experience when purpose and meaning resonate with each individual and with the group as a whole. CR is thinking individually and collectively simultaneously and being individual and collective simultaneously. In early years community development, CR occurs when an individual has discovered the relevance and meaning of their participation in the collaborative — and begins to look beyond that to see what is relevant for others in the collaborative, in the community, and how it benefits children.

We scoured the literature, read books from many disciplines, and searched high and low for descriptions that might inform our emerging understanding of CR. We were inspired by many authors and relieved to find we weren't the only ones wrestling with the words to describe this advanced concept in group dynamics.

Following is a compilation of collaborative terms and descriptions that provide a useful summary of some of the "big thinking" that exists in the areas of teamwork and collaboration. We suggest you read more about the terms that intrigue you or resonate with your experiences. Talk about these, and the concept of CR, with other people. The terms and concepts provide information and tools that can open up conversations and lead to greater collaborative growth. We've added some questions to think about, ones that helped us wrap our heads around the applicability of these concepts in early years community development.

This table is evidence — from the thinking of many brilliant minds (and the many others out there) — that when individuals authentically connect, "something more" emerges.

CONCEPT	SUMMARY	AUTHOR	Something to think about . . .
Aggregation	The term "aggregation"' implies viewing everything in a larger context — everything is interconnected. It reflects the underlying system behind everyone and everything.	Motwane, (2000), *The power of wisdom*	How is aggregation different from integration?
Alignment	Alignment is behaviours, beliefs, values, identities, spirits, and strengths lining up. These may not be the same or in common but are heading in the same direction, complementing and adding to one another.	Joyce (2007), *Teaching an anthill to fetch*	How can groups find alignment in diversity?
Collective Effervescence	Collective Effervescence is a natural byproduct of the patterns of interaction that occur between people. These patterns generate energy by sharing a common idea and a common sense of purpose leading to "sentiments that excite participants to the point of frenzy and awaken the sensation of the sacred and divine."	Durkheim (1976), *Elementary forms of the religious life*	Do you have to "give up" differences to achieve collective effervescence?\n\nWhat role does spirituality have in collective experiences?
Community Transformation	Transformation of a large number of individual people does *not* result in the transformation of communities. It is the shift in mindset about our connectedness that brings about transformation.	Block (2008), *Community: The structure of belonging*	How do we choose to be together?\n\nWhat do we want to create together?

Continuum of Inter- agency Efforts	Cooperation, coordination, and collaboration can be viewed as a continuum. Where an interagency group sits depends on the extent and nature of interdependent relationships between agencies, with collaboration being highly interdependent and cooperation being more independent.	Goldman & Intrilligator (1990), Factors that enhance collaboration among education, health and social service agencies	Is there a relationship beyond collaboration? Where does your collaborative want to be on the continuum? Have you talked about it? Is the relationship goal different for different issues?
Emergence	When separate, local efforts connect with each other as networks, a surprisingly new system suddenly emerges on a greater scale. This system of influence possesses qualities and capacities that were unknown in the individuals.	Wheatley & Frieze (2006), Using emergence to take social innovation to scale	What are the benefits of connecting networks within a community, within neighbouring communities, and/or across the globe? How could this be accomplished?
Social Innovation	Social innovation gets partners working together to a higher-order purpose on complex challenges to achieve breakthrough results. Every person contributes what they can and makes a difference, but no one person can claim responsibility for the result.	Westley, Zimmerman & Patton (2006), *Getting to maybe*	What is your collaborative's higher-order purpose? Are breakthrough results always tangible?
Synergy	Synergy, broadly defined, refers to combined or "cooperative" effects — literally, the effects produced by things (parts, elements, or individuals) that "operate together." The term is frequently associated with the slogan "the whole is greater than the sum of its parts," which traces back to Aristotle.	Corning (1983), *The synergism hypothesis*	What situations would you attribute to synergy?

The Integral Capacity Building Framework	An integral map shows four dimensions in which community development and planning are carried out and how these dimensions are interconnected. The integral approach provides a more detailed map of the contexts in which collaboration is carried out. (See example below.)	BC Healthy Communities (2006)	What happens when all four quadrants are balanced? Does the group magic happen when there is an imbalance?
The Theory of the U	The U theory suggests a different process of "co-creation" between the individual or collective and the larger world. The self and the world are inescapably interconnected.	Senge, Scharmer, Jaworski & Flowers (2005), *Presence*	Has your collaborative thought about its role in co-creation with issues beyond young children?

THE SMALL VILLAGE DISCOVERS A STATE OF COLLECTIVE RELEVANCE

Let's seek that something more — the magic — through our little social masters, who will shed some light on what it means to experience Collective Relevance.

When we last left the small village, the educator was working on involving all four children by comparing the height of the blocks to each person.

This personal interaction stops Tanner in his tracks. Interested, he places another block on top of the structure and presses his body close to the tower to see if he is, indeed, taller than the stacked blocks.

Morgan is paying close attention to Tanner's actions. She stands up to take a closer look, which intrigues Brynn as well, bringing both girls closer to the action. Grace is watching.

All four children take turns comparing themselves with the blocks. This action brings out a feeling of commonality — something they can all be a part of and all understand.

After this moment of measuring, Tanner brings the group

AN INTEGRAL MAP OF COMMUNITY

THE INNER INDIVIDUAL	THE OUTER INDIVIDUAL
PSYCHOLOGICAL & SPIRITUAL • Awareness, thought, feeling • Attitudes, values, beliefs, intentions • Inner health & well-being, self-esteem • Sense of safety, trust • Sense of connectedness, responsibility & caring–for others and the environment • Creativity, innovation, artistic expression • Motivation & experience of participation & contribution	PHYSICAL & BEHAVIORAL • Physical health and well-being • Skills & abilities • Activities • Program participation • Consumer behaviours • Diet, fitness • Actions toward others and the environment • Skills and opportunities for participation & contribution
CULTURAL • Worldviews • Shared meaning • Collective norms, ethics • Shared attitudes, values, beliefs • Shared vision & goals • Stories, myths • Shared history, customs • Shared language, symbols, art • Co-creativity • Culture of participation & contribution	NATURAL SYSTEMS/SOCIAL SYSTEMS • Natural environment, ecological systems • Built environment, human systems • Community institutions (schools, health, authority, justice system, religious institutions, etc.) • Programs and services • Laws, policies, protocols • Organizational systems & structures • Community infrastructure (transportation, housing, social planning council, etc.) • Governance systems & structures • Economic system • Systems & structures for participation & contribution
THE INNER COLLECTIVE	THE OUTER COLLECTIVE

back to the task at hand. He throws out a challenge to the now closely knit team.

"How about we make our castle bigger?" he says. "How will we make it bigger? We don't have any more blocks."

That's all it takes. Whether it was the moment of finding an activity they could all take part in (the measuring) or whether it was simply having more time together, the group now appears ready to resume the building.

Grace runs away and exclaims in a deep, excited voice, "I've got my blocks from my little castle."

Tanner jumps on the opportunity to acquire more building materials and grabs blocks from Grace's structure, one in each hand.

Grace freezes beside her structure, tense and frowning, unsure of this new stage of development. She's engaged in the teamwork, but not necessarily ready to contribute her personal resources or for others to be taking the blocks.

The educator notices Grace's reaction and with a respectful question asks the group, "Should we ask Grace?" This question provides an opportunity for Grace to express how she feels.

"No, that's *my* castle," she says, reaching out to take one of the blocks from Tanner.

Tanner takes the remaining block back to the larger structure — every block counts! Grace replaces the other block back on top of her castle and stands in front of her work, unsettled at the threat to her blocks.

The educator acknowledges how Grace is feeling and states, "Grace worked really hard on her structure." She turns to Grace and says, "You're right." This gives Grace more time to consider what to do next.

Morgan is watching Grace.

Brynn is still building the larger structure with Tanner.

The educator passes Morgan a block to engage her in the play at the larger structure.

Brynn stands on top of another block to place a new block up high. When the block falls off, she shrieks with excitement — definitely warming up to this building activity.

Tanner, still looking for additional building resources, complains under his breath, "We still need more blocks."

Only seconds have passed but that is all the time Grace needs. She is now ready to knock down her tower and share her blocks. She has heard Tanner and carries her blocks to the larger village.

Tanner eyes the fallen blocks like a child lined up at a dessert buffet, but he respects Grace's need for space. He does not go to the pile . . . yet. All four children are now chatting and building together.

The educator takes this opportunity to say, "Do you know what I see happening here? Teamwork!"

Morgan speaks the loudest we have heard thus far: "We can go through this." Then she shows everyone a way to enter the castle.

Brynn has moved to the outside of the group while the other three continue building.

The excitement is contagious.

"There are more blocks over here," Grace announces to the group. She is ready for the others to gather and use her materials.

Tanner has been waiting for this moment. He leaps with giant strides across the room to pick up Grace's blocks for inclusion in the bigger castle, thrilled at the bounty of building materials.

The educator asks Morgan and Brynn, "Should we help Grace bring them over?"

Morgan and Brynn join in the convoy of blocks. Grace works double-time, rushing back and forth to dump the blocks closer to the bigger castle, still feeling her connection to the blocks but now eager to contribute them. Her face glows with pride.

Slowly the individual builders have merged, taking their individual resources and creating something new. They all feel connected to the larger group castle — perhaps moving from individual to collective relevance.

Ask yourself: *If I were Grace and her block structure was my organization's program, how would I feel? Would I be protective and hesitant?*

How does the story change if the blocks are funding or human resources? Where in the story do you sense the "magic" for the group?

MAKING BEAUTIFUL
HARMONY

*"After silence, that which comes nearest to
expressing the inexpressible is music."*
— ALDOUS HUXLEY, *MUSIC AT NIGHT*

Music is one of those media that help us put feelings into
words. Harmony is a commonly used analogy for describing
the powerful and special connections that exist in group experiences,
synergies, and moments.

In her book *The Tao of Personal Leadership*, Diane Dreher uses a
music analogy to celebrate how our differences make organizations
stronger. Although no two voices are exactly alike, they can "flow
together to create deeper, more beautiful patterns than any one voice
could create alone" (Dreher, 1996, p. 38). The harmony that individual voices create together is something new, but individuals must
maintain their individuality to make it work. If the voices sound like
copies of one other, the result will be a droning hum. When individuals

and organizations can be both individual and collective at the same time — let the music begin.

We have participated in several experiences in which a group of people (who giggled and blushed because they never sing outside the shower, if then) learned how to create the most beautiful, scalp-tingling three-part harmony. The music, in this case, was more than an analogy: It was a successful collaborative experience that clearly demonstrated the feeling of CR.

Keith Sawyer (2007) spent significant time doing research on improvisational theatre and jazz combo groups. He looked specifically at the group dynamics and outcomes of the creative power of collaboration. He hypothesized that the qualities musicians put into the process of creating music are those we can learn from and apply to other parts of our lives, such as our business relations. He found that the best inspiration for collaboration comes when members play off one another, each person's contributions providing the spark for the next.

Just like a jazz jam session, then, early years community development is the combination of everyone's individuality. CR happens when individuals see how their contributions can become part of something larger than themselves or their organizations, when they see how the work can become relevant on many levels. The focus transcends what's in it for me or for us to be on what's in it for the three Cs: the children, the community, and the collaborative. To see collective relevance, one must see the bigger picture: the whole.

THE STICKY STORY

TAMMY
One night while deep into my research for *Raising the Village*, I sat and digested the pages of what seemed like the seventy-second community development book of the week surrounded by packages of mini sticky notes. I was using them to earmark the pages that I thought would be useful to my composition. I was preoccupied and on a personal deadline.

I'm embarrassed to say that when my daughter asked if she could cuddle up to me and help put the stickies on the pages, I was not an eager, open-hearted mother. Let's admit it, researching with an inquisitive four-year-old nearby is like trying to shovel your walkway while it's still snowing.

I was about to unleash my super-mom abilities to distract her, but something inside told me to pause: to take a moment and see her interest and involvement as a gift. I took a deep breath, and said, with all my heart, "Sure, I could use your help!" Her obvious pleasure filled me with instant warmth — but I got even more out of our interaction than I expected.

As we sat side by side on the couch, my usually talkative daughter was fairly quiet. Though she wiggled and danced as she organized the colourful stickies into a fan shape on the table, her attention was mainly on watching me read. When I paused, she knew it was time to pull a sticky off the coffee table and insert it on the page. We worked together like this for all 475 pages of the book.

When I finally closed the book, I was relaxed and content, thrilled to have completed a project with my four-year-old. I looked at the all the many-coloured stickies and reflected with satisfaction on the many rewarding connections they promised.

My daughter was just as happy and proud of her work as assistant sticky person to Mom. She gazed at the book and exclaimed, "Wow! What a beautiful book!"

I was puzzled. What a beautiful book? I looked again and saw it as my daughter did. She wasn't thinking of what was in the passages I had marked but of something else altogether. Even though the stickies layered the book in a haphazard fashion, together they made an aesthetically pleasing, vibrantly coloured masterpiece.

The lesson for me was immediate: to appreciate individual richness and at the same time to look at the beauty that lies when the random pieces mingle. Somehow the untidy, coloured scraps worked together and, sticky by sticky, created a bigger, fuller, more beautiful picture.

HOW TO DO IT? DO MORE OF IT BY . . .

Moving from independent work to collaborative work is not a quick and easy leap. It is often misunderstood and translated into lofty goals and objectives that feel forced and an attempt to impose structure on something that is essentially magic. When individuals and organizations are connected and form a collective, they maintain their individuality, strengths, and autonomy.

In *The Art of Facilitation*, Hunter, Bailey & Taylor (1995) describe five levels that groups evolve through as they approach CR.

The first is when a group's physical needs are taken care of.

This is followed by a level of thinking in which ideas are shared, creative thinking exists, inspiration happens, and there is less complaining and more contribution.

The third level is emotional. Participants own the emotions and feelings behind their motivations. What happens comes from the heart and contributes to trust building.

In the fourth level (the intuitive level), a group feels they are onto something: A common chord is struck.

Finally, according to these authors, comes the synergistic level, characterized by a change in group energy. This is the level of transformation. Group members become aware that they are at one, that they are aligned and attuned. People start to notice one another in a new way, judgments are suspended, and spontaneity is accessed.

Is CR measurable? Is it something you feel, or is it an objective group outcome? Can you feel a little CR? Sure you can. Can you feel knocked off your feet with CR? Sure you can. But how do you know? If you feel it, it's there.

CR is working, thinking, seeing, and feeling together in a variety of ways. Our practical approach to helping people work toward CR is dialogue. Specifically, we create a space, ask phenomenological questions, and add generous amounts of creativity.

DIALOGUE

*"Our heritage and ideals,
our codes and standards —
the things we live by and teach our
children — are preserved or diminished
by how freely we exchange ideas and feelings."*
— WALT DISNEY

In an age in which there are too many things to do and brevity and dismal spelling are excused because the communicator is texting on a phone the size of a small piece of toast, taking the time to talk to others tends to be overlooked.

Even among families and neighbours, time spent talking is diminished because of the decline of activities that once got us out and about in the community. Now we shop online, seek entertainment from our home theatres, and plug into MP3 players.

Very few families sit down to eat dinner together — another lost opportunity to talk. Yet as Werner Erhard, who introduced the concept of social transformation in the 1970s, has put it, any kind of transformation (for example raising a village) is actually a linguistic task. It has to involve talking (Block, 2008).

Talking to each other isn't such a useful piece of guidance on its own, but we have taken this key concept and broken it down into practices that are suitable for early years community development. After significant experimentation with facilitation techniques and group work, we have experienced that to authentically and effectively get people talking, thoughtful dialogue opportunities must be offered. In particular, two aspects of dialogue that work in early years community development include creating space and the use of phenomenological questions — both of which mean talking.

Dialogue is an opportunity to create shared meaning, to learn from each member of the group, and to jointly explore an issue. The result is not a decision, an action plan, or an agreement: It is simply a deeper shared understanding (Bohm, Factor & Garrett, 1991). Dialogue is very different from discussion or debate, the latter of which includes both problem-solving and seeking closure to an issue. In stark contrast, dialogue "seeks to open possibilities and see new options" (Isaacs, 1999, p. 45). It is an exploration and creation aimed at reaching new, collective understanding. The word "dialogue" comes from the root words *dia* (meaning through) and *logos* (the word). Dialogue, then, gives the image "of a river of meaning flowing around and through each participant" (Bohm et al., 1991, p. 4).

Child development is actually used as an analogy by Isaacs (1999) to explain the complexity and multiplicity of factors that influence dialogue. Noting that energy, possibility, and safety are three critical qualities required for the healthy growth and development of children, Isaacs asks whether there is "energy, possibility and safety" in the place where you want to develop important conversations or co-create meaning. Dialogue offers a process that promotes energy and possibility and can be managed to provide the safety required for people to contribute fully.

CREATING THE SPACE

Dialogue isn't going to happen without some thought and attention to creating a space that is conducive to Isaacs' triumvirate of energy, possibility, and safety. He writes about creating space as setting the container to avoid doubt, confusion, and lack of trust among participants. "The idea behind the container is that human beings need a setting in which to hold the intensities of their lives" (Isaacs, 1999, p. 227). It is a space designed to suspend judgments and promote fresh perspectives. It requires attention both to the physical place and facilitated experience.

The ultimate place for dialogue to occur is one that is welcoming, relaxed, and completely separate from any one participant's "turf." While we don't always have access to ideal places, the physical arrangement of a setting can always be adjusted. Chairs can be placed in a circle, plants can soften a formal décor, and people or signs can welcome participants into the room.

Once the participants enter this space, facilitating the experience is critical to maintaining and promoting authentic sharing and mutual learning. Skilled facilitators work to guide the group conversations and are responsive to the group dynamics that arise. Conflict, misunderstandings, and territorialism are all possible but can be kept at bay when the playing field is kept level, the group guidelines are clear, and the atmosphere is positive.

Collective relevance occurs when individuals push to a deep hearing of others in order to deepen connections. Make sure every participant has an opportunity to actively share their thoughts. Decisions and actions will then be owned by the participants. When people can see how they assist in meeting the goals and objectives of the collaborative, even though the result may not entirely reflect their individual thought, they grasp how they are represented in the collective decision because the dialogue reflects everyone.

Spaces for dialogue don't have to look the same every time. Following are some ideas to frame and support talking time.

• *Location:* A few of the most moving meeting moments we have facilitated or participated in occurred in our own homes. Hosting a meeting within the intimate, welcoming walls of your home may not always be appropriate, but there are times when a topic may be better suited to an informal setting rather than the typical boardroom. Consider the topic of spirituality and First Nations culture and traditions. Convening around a boardroom table somehow fails to bring pictures to mind of spiritual and cultural sharing — although it can be done there, too. Other examples in which the location added to the ambience of the meeting include meetings outdoors for year-end celebrations and meals, a rotation of meetings at various organizations' worksites, and research/literature discussions at coffee shops. Be mindful of locations that can stimulate and provoke dialogue.

• *Internal knowledge:* Using collaborative members as guest speakers and using internal knowledge are ways not only to build capacity but also to create a different energy in a meeting space. Just imagine Cathy, who has attended collaborative meetings for five years. She has built up camaraderie and relationships with the members. Therefore, engagement of the other collaborative members is enhanced when she suddenly presents at a meeting and shares her expertise in asset building. Acknowledging the knowledge and strengths in the room is a wonderful way to create an animated group environment.

• *Flexible Agendas:* It's budget determination time and the collaborative has more ideas than money. The ideas are not new. They have been floating from meeting to meeting for months but the facilitators, despite the time pressure of fiscal accountability, sense that participants are not quite ready to commit to a priority. The opportunity for dialogue whips into the room like a full-force gale. With an openness to flexibility in the agenda, the facilitators stop in mid-budget discussion and focus instead on helping the participants create a better understanding for themselves of what they need to explore and learn before making any decisions.

• *Sharing a Meal:* Snow is gently falling outside the meeting room. Collaborative participants arrive to the welcoming scents of casseroles, fruit salad, and baked goodies and the pleasing view of well-dressed tables set for a meal. Participants join small tables of four or five people and share a meal — brunch, in this case — while they launch into personal sharing.

They are asked to:
  • Share a time when a non-family member adult made a difference in their life.
  • Discuss how this experience influenced whom they have become.
  • Explore the question of how they are a significant adult in a young child's life now.

Aboriginal colleagues and friends have taught us that a space with food nourishes both the people and the work, allowing the messages to be digested.

• *Using Props and Tools:* Talking sticks, stones, magic wands, and rope are examples of props that can help to create a space for sharing. As a participant is passed a stone, he absently feels its smooth texture and heaviness. It grounds him to take the time — uninterrupted time — to share thoughts and ideas. The stone signals a sense of respect with its presence ensuring that every voice is heard. When it is offered to others, they may choose to take it and add their voice to the dialogue or pass it along while they continue to listen.

• *Individual Reflection:* With flip-chart paper taped across the front of the room and a quiver full of colourful markers, the facilitator introduces the task of brainstorming to generate ideas on the topic at hand. Brainstorming is a common technique that can be helpful to launch deeper dialogue fuelled by the volumes of rich information that are generated. Before beginning the brainstorm, however, the participants are asked to take a few minutes for individual reflection. They take some time to assess their perceptions, assumptions, and passions on the topic at hand before the group energy sweeps into the work. They are then well armed to enter into the dialogue that follows with thoughts that are grounded with their own inner voice.

Yankelovich (1999) writes that the act of collaboration must start with dialogue because you cannot build relationships without having an understanding of your potential partners, and you cannot achieve that understanding without a special form of communication that goes beyond the ordinary conversation. David Bohm, considered one of the founding thinkers of the dialogue movement, writes that trust between group members and trust in a group process will "lead to the expression of the sorts of thoughts and feelings that are usually kept hidden" (Bohm et al., 1991, p. 6). With trust and communication cultivated in the dialogue process, the odds of successful collaboration increase.

PHENOMENOLOGICAL QUESTIONS

Peter Block (2008) says that questions demand engagement and that engagement, in turn, creates accountability. What better ingredients for change than engagement and accountability? Not just any question will do. Block goes on to write that we define our future through the questions we choose to address. Well-crafted and mindfully placed questions can be an invitation for engagement, hook people ready to take ownership of the future, awaken possibilities, explore doubts and dissention, solidify commitment, and celebrate the strengths we have to offer one another along the way.

The question has to matter, too. If the "answers" are too easy or obvious then the question is wrong. Evoke some reaction: Cause people to think about themselves, their values, and their behaviours. In an age of quick fixes and rushaholism, there is added motivation to make the limited opportunities that we do have for dialogue to be as meaningful as possible. This means asking phenomenological questions: ones aimed at understanding and sharing the meaning of our experiences. These questions push the edge to help us understand ourselves and how we interact. An element of risk goes a long way to ensure meaningful dialogue, trust building, and connections. Children, our greatest teachers, do this well. They use questions to explore their world.

Why, how, and what are the most powerful question starters. They avoid yes or no answers, they get beyond the facts generated by when and where questions, and they get to deeper reflective thinking. Phenomenological questions are vague enough that people have to stretch their thinking to give some meaning to it. They need to work to relate the question to their feelings and experiences.

SAMPLE PHENOMENOLOGICAL QUESTIONS

These are a sampling of our top ten favourite questions (Vogt, Brown & Isaacs, 2003; Block, 2008):

- What could happen that would enable you/us to feel fully engaged and energized about (your issue)?
- What question, if answered, could make the most difference to the future of (your issue)?
- To what extent do you see yourself as a cause of the problem you are trying to fix?
- What is the story you carry about this issue? What are the payoffs and costs to maintaining this story?
- What is missing from this picture so far? What is it we are not seeing? What do we need more clarity about?

- What are the strengths/gifts you hold that have not been brought out fully?
- What promises are you willing to make to your peers?
- If our success was completely guaranteed, what bold steps might we choose?
- What is emerging here for you? What new connections are you making?
- What gifts have you received from others?

One danger in asking a question is that it may elicit advice. A well-crafted question will eliminate advice as a response, replacing it with a spirit of inquiry: a response that is relevant, curious, and challenges assumptions. Questions that generate hope, imagination, creative action, and engagement release energy to imagine possibilities and construct workable approaches.

Confession time! Every once in a while a question is posed to a group and it doesn't elicit meaningful dialogue — in fact, it bombs! There are often hopes and expectations behind deep questions, and unfortunately, and for a variety of reasons, things may fall flat. Perhaps there is not enough time provided to get anywhere, perhaps there are trust issues that become barriers for sharing, perhaps the phenomenological question, carefully worded in preparation, is unclear, is too complicated, or just plain misses the mark.

It's not easy to create dialogue and craft the questions that start them. In particular, personal and edgy questions need a great deal of context. Participants need to be comfortable and given permission to share unpopular answers, be a voice of dissension, and add diversity to dialogue with some healthy conflict.

By learning together and posing phenomenological questions to each other and ourselves, we help ourselves better understand our present and possible futures. The authors of the book *Presence* ask, "What question lies at the heart of your work?" (Senge et al., 2005, p. 11). We would like to add: What questions lie beneath why people come together over an issue? What questions motivate them to stay? And what questions keep bringing them back? The questions themselves have more power than answers.

SPACE, DIALOGUE . . . AND CR

What triggers collective relevance? What inspires innovation and vision in groups? What makes working together fun? Allowing creative juices to run! Creativity is an indispensable part of dialogue, creating space and phenomenological questions. There is no better way to think outside the box or to tackle complex issues then to encourage the creative imagination and inventiveness of each collaborative member.

As Dan B. Allender establishes in his book *Leading with a Limp*, "creativity finds its best soil in the dirt of chaos . . . If we want something better than one 'right' way, we must seek input of people who will help us find a different path from the one we would come up with on our own . . . This is not an exercise in seeking consensus. We don't manage complexity by coming to the perfect and unanimously approved plan before we move forward. But true creativity requires risk as the precondition for a new harmony to rise" (Allender, 2006, p. 91).

How do we increase creativity as a way to experience CR more often? We encourage you to blaze your own creative path and look for opportunities to flip, reframe, or expand discussion in group situations by initiating some type of creative response or approach. Here are a few ideas we have tried:

- Create a mission statement using champagne glasses with sparkling orange juice. Really! Break people into partners tasked with designing a toast for the early years collaborative. In turn, take these toasts and synthesize them into a mission statement.
- Try inventive ways to conduct strategic planning. How about a strategic plan scavenger hunt — yes, another true story!
- Use a variety of facilitation props and tools to expand conversations and break away from flip-chart recording. How about

having pipe cleaners on the table, or graffiti walls, or creating sculptures with tinfoil to express an idea.

- Humour — let your quirks and personality shine.
- Look at things from different perspectives. We have used a devil's trident to encourage examining the devil's advocate perspective. We have also developed a process to "flip the coin," forcing participants to brainstorm from the other side of the coin.

Even the great Leonardo da Vinci looked at his ideas and created his inventions by drawing them from many perspectives. By doing so, he expanded his understanding and learning. By consciously looking at issues from multiple perspectives, and at the same time expanding all of the group's perspectives, we can better understand any issues, any possible solutions or actions, and any potential implications — and have fun while we're doing it.

ACTIVITY #10

GIVE/GET

General Idea
Hold give/get conversations to increase personal relevance between individuals and the early years collaborative.

What's Worked for Us . . .
STEP 1
Self-reflection: What do you give and what do you get out of your involvement with a collaborative? Make a list.

GIVE	GET

STEP 2

Share individual responses in small groups. Listen to each other and ask questions. Any surprises? Commonalities? Differences? Gather ideas from the groups on how to use group strengths most effectively to meet the group needs.

STEP 3

Create a collective list from the individual lists. Hold further dialogue to inform a large-group plan.

OUR COLLECTIVE GIVE/GET

ACTIVITY #11

INTERVIEW MATRIX

General Idea

First introduced to us by our colleague Chris Gay, this activity is an innovative and inclusive way for people to share ideas. At first glance, the process may seem complicated, but our directions make things clear. It works best when you have a minimum of twelve people to a maximum of sixty.

What's Worked for Us . . .

STEP 1

Craft four questions. Relate the questions to the task at hand: visioning, action priorities, professional learning, or whatever is needed. Use the following format as a guide:

What are two or three things that _____?

(e.g., help us meet our goals)

What are two or three things that _____?

(e.g., are barriers to achieve our goals)

What are two or three things that _____?

(e.g., we need to move forward)

What are two or three things that _____?

(e.g., we need to stop doing)

STEP 2

Begin by having people form groups of four. Provide each participant with a handout (see below) and assign each person a letter from *a* to *d*. Follow the interview schedule listed on the next page:

a interviews b while c interviews d
b interviews a while d interviews c
b interviews c while d interviews a
c interviews b while a interviews d
a interviews c while b interviews d
c interviews a while d interviews b

STEP 3

There are a total of twelve interviews in six time slots. Each person will interview the three other people in their group, and each person will be personally interviewed by the other three people. The rhythm is fast paced. Each interview is only three minutes long — don't go over the time! Switch interviews quickly at the end of each three-minute slot.

STEP 4

When the interviewing is complete, form a group for each letter. Let the people for that letter share and compare their findings from their interview question.

STEP 5

Ask each small group to report back about common themes that emerged.

INTERVIEW MATRIX WORKSHEET

Your letter:

Your question:

Instructions:

You always ask the same question.

Listen for directions regarding whom you interview next and when others are to interview you.

Please write down everything that the person you are interviewing says.

Responses to your first interview:

Responses to your second interview:

Responses to your third interview:

ACTIVITY #12

THE HUNT

General Idea

"The hunt" is a form of celebration that provides a summary of the group's accomplishments and future goals. As well as providing a fun way for people to participate in and connect to the collective action plan, this activity is an effective team builder. The hunt is full of potential to further deepen group relationships and relevance while engaging in a playful way.

What's Worked for Us . . .

STEP 1

Design a scavenger hunt that directly relates to the work of the early years collaborative. Our example follows — but be creative and customize your hunt to fit your group.

Bringing Strategic Action Alive ~
Make Children First Network Scavenger Hunt

Team Two: THE HUNT! Find the following:

- A photo of a "Family Friendly Business"

- A picture of the City's official Seal (bonus for a photo of a city official)

- An Alberni Valley map: circle the locations of the MCFN partners (as many as you can)

- Something in nature that represents "celebration"

- A photo of someone you stopped on the street to tell about MCFN

- A picture of something you would like to see on the website

- Bonus Riddle: "All along the mountains and sea"...whoever could I be?

Back at the Park!

- As a team find your hidden piece of foil. Now using the foil create a "sculpture" which represents a highlight from the past year or a vision for 2008.

- Reflection Card: Make your own team reflection card with hidden quotes, photos and art hiding in the park.

- Review the yearly meeting feedback sheets. Pull out one item that your group would like to include in our Strategic Action or discuss further in the Fall.

- You have 20 minutes for the park activities. Work together to get it done. You will report back your journey to the larger group.

PART 5

SUSTAINING THE VILLAGE

14

STRENGTHS ARE A DIFFERENT WAY OF THINKING

"When we seek to discover the best in others, we somehow bring out the best in ourselves."
— WILLIAM ARTHUR WARD

Sustainability is a buzz word that means different things to different people. For some it means sustainable resources and funding. For others it means succession planning. For yet others it may signify longevity and long-term collaborative success. For early years community development, sustainability is all of the above, plus it nurtures the three village-raising strategies toward a consistent development of personal and collective strengths.

What does that mean? It means that as individuals, organizations, and a collective, we do our work by contributing what makes us strong. We consistently find purpose and passion in what we choose to create and what we choose to engage, how we choose to interact with one another, and how we participate when the rubber hits the road. The late Donald Clifton, father of the strengths movement and a scientist with the Gallup Organization, asked the question, "What would happen if we studied what was right with people versus what was wrong?"(Clifton & Nelson, 1995, p. 20).

Over a period of forty years, the Gallup Organization identified the thirty-four most common human talents. These talents show up in our work lives and our personal lives. Their research results also found that having the opportunity to develop individual strengths plays a critical role in work and life success.

In early years community development, we can apply this knowledge and translate it at both an individual level and at a group level within collaboratives. When we focus on the early years and intentionally work from a place of strength, we have a greater chance of positive outcomes and can, we believe, better sustain collaboration.

WHAT IS A STRENGTH?

Most people's lives are so full these days with work, family, and even recreational demands that it feels to them as if the critically important stuff of life — like going to the dentist, spending quality time with a friend, or fitting in a bedtime story — are "off the side of the desk." Maybe it's time to redefine our desks, marrying every square inch of them to our individual strengths, skills, and passions so that we are at our most effective, most productive, and happiest. Internationally acclaimed author and strengths consultant Marcus Buckingham teaches people to recognize their strengths and apply them in their lives. "Your strengths are the specific activities that *make you feel strong*" (Buckingham, 2008, p. 43).

THE DREAM CATCHER

TAMMY
"I think our group would be even better if the girls felt like they had more control."

This straight-shooting comment came from a teen parent who was part of the parent support group that I facilitated in a child-care centre. Quite frankly, I was unsure what to do with this advice. I sat with the feedback for a moment and then asked for clarification.

"Tell me more about what you mean by control," I asked.

"Well, we are already controlled so much in our lives. We are often told what to do or feel judged by others. I just think we would be into the groups more if we had more control over the group itself."

"Well put!" I said.

At the next weekly meeting of the young parent group I started a conversation with specific questions, such as: "What would you like to share with each other? How can we share things that matter to us — things that interest us?"

The group was fairly quiet, contemplating the various questions until one girl spoke up.

"I can make dream catchers."

"Awesome! What do you like about making dream catchers?" I asked.

The young parent told the group how it was an important part of her culture and how she had made a special dream catcher to hang above her child's crib to ward off bad dreams and bring restful sleep.

This intimate disclosure of parental love was enough to get the group's ideas flowing. One by one, the participants expressed areas that fired them up — the sharing was phenomenal.

It was decided that parents would take one of the weekly meetings and, with me as guide, plan the group. The resulting groups were strength-filled and based on personal meaning. I was humbled by the rich and thoughtful planning of the parents.

One parent wrote a poem about the love she had for her child and read it to the group, spurring the discussion for the day. Another parent courageously recited details of her traumatic, yet hope-filled life story, which she took hours to write and shared with pride and courage.

Yet another felt that teen parents received a bad rap and that so many groups were based on "teaching people how to parent" or focused on negative issues such as substance abuse, that she wanted to craft a group session on positive parenting. This parent shared local resources and inspirational quotes and poems, and she shared from her heart what she found positive about being a young parent.

Another parent went to several parks in the community and reported back what she saw as the pros and cons of each one.

And yes, the group crafted dream catchers filled with colour and love for their children. As the young parent leading the group that day instructed others how to weave and twine the materials around the rim, she sparkled with confidence. The opportunity to teach her skill in crafting with the other parents gave her new strength and belief in herself and her talents.

Think not of the things you do well but of the things you are proud of, the things that instinctively put a spring in your step or a song in your heart. Anything that brings you enthusiasm or passion is something to pay attention to and share with others. The dream-catcher story helps to illustrate that in any group, when participants have the opportunity to share their strengths, the group as a whole benefits. Consider how strengths can be brought forward more intentionally in your early years collaborative.

FOCUS ON STRENGTHS

William Damon (2006) states that it is never too early to begin a life of purpose, and never too late. Purpose is grounded in who you are and what you have to give — essentially your strengths. Strengths and purpose are found everywhere but often are most meaningful when found in familiar places. For example, strengths are the things you already do that fill you with energy and drive whether they be job activities, your hobbies, or your interactions with family and friends. Your strengths cannot be found in a job-performance measurement or be identified by anyone other than you. The truth of self-discovery is that the only person who knows what makes you tick is you.

With that in mind, we shudder at some of the theories that exist on the subject of strengths.

A close colleague shared his experience of "strengths training" as part of an organizational retreat in which his boss chose a strength for each employee and wrote that strength on a sticky note. He then placed the note on the employee's forehead without allowing them to see it. Our friend had the humiliating experience of having to mingle with his team and talk with others about their strengths, each not knowing what was written on their own heads until the end. Crazy but true: This experiential activity, using "strengths" in this way, resulted in tears and being judged on things outside their control.

Other stories include strength "inventories," often a tool or questionnaire. These can leave people feeling graded or pressured to excel at something they don't necessarily enjoy doing. This type of labelling almost gives licence to people to pigeonhole others using a colour, symbol, or set of letters, relegating them to having just two or three talents.

Most activities that help people and teams explore strengths do not intend to cause these reactions, but the danger is inherent in them.

Similarly, in an early years collaborative, the group's strengths cannot be labelled and found in a list in a book or a government funder's report, or in a sell job to get more money. They are created within and discovered by the group itself. Sustaining early years community development involves knowing and harnessing the strengths of the village. This intentional activity will be at its most effective when the strengths of the group drive, move, and create a future for the group.

In order to do this, we must think in a new way. We must think in a strengths paradigm. As Peter Senge (2005) describes it, the process is one of untying the ropes that individually and collectively prevent us from moving forward together. Think not of limits, weaknesses, gaps, and threats, but of what we have that will move us forward.

UNTAPPED POTENTIAL

The Relevance Survey in chapter 10 was a tool we used in our work with an early years collaborative. One question, in particular, evoked surprising responses: To what extent are we, as a collaborative, aware of and utilizing the strengths and skills of all participants? The responses were:

- 3.8% not at all
- 57.7% a fair amount
- 38.5% a great extent.

This information tipped us off to untapped potential within the collaborative. Over time the collaborative embarked further on the strength development of each member, in the hopes of reinforcing the relationships, leadership, and relevance that already existed. Some of the actions included strength-inspired conversations, journals, and group processes. The group went so far as to formalize the strengths way of working together into the collaborative's orientation and information packages.

The group was asked how it could use its collective strengths and new strength knowledge. Responses included:

- Explore strengths within our organizations.
- Apply strengths in preparing for job interviews and funding applications.
- Help each other explore strengths by looking at them in depth.
- Validate what each participant brings to the table.

HICCUPS AND BUMPS

Sustaining any kind of momentum is hard work because in the real world roadblocks inhibit collaboration, diminish creativity, and stop innovation in its tracks. It is very common for community initiatives of every kind to fizzle out.

Looking at strengths from both an individual and collective perspective can help us sustain the efforts of a collaborative. Hold a "common language" discussion to investigate how working together with strengths keeps the "something larger than ourselves" at the forefront.

A strength focus helps us to reframe and see each situation differently, minimizing the inevitable hiccups and bumps along the way. The following story shows just how strengths can be used to reframe conflict.

CHALLENGES OR STRENGTHS?

It's movie day. A group of early years collaborative participants are *not* gathered around a boardroom table. Instead they are sipping coffee and tea perched on comfortable sofas in the comfort of the facilitator's home. Fellowship and goodwill fill the air. The group is prepared to devote an entire morning's discussion to what makes them feel strong as a collective. Not a bad day's work!

The movie lighting up the screen is an inspirational, informative movie by Marcus Buckingham (2006), *Trombone Player Wanted*. When it ends, sharing begins. It doesn't take long to get into an authentic conversation. You know the kind, where the room goes still and someone has the courage to speak a personal truth.

We can recognize these truths in many ways: a tremble in the voice, a sense of discovery in a person's eyes, or emotion-filled words that hang in the air.

In this case, two people share that they thought their strengths had been misunderstood. They felt their contributions were unwelcome when they raised cautions during meetings because they went against the flow.

The other members in the room are also able to reach a new place of awareness. They see that these two people were sharing their strengths when they focused on cautions rather than possibilities. What first appear as challenges can be reframed as strengths.

This type of reframing can also be applied to other difficult situations. A group can get to the root of conflict with deep listening, taking time to see and hear multiple perspectives and reflecting as a group centred on strengths. The familiar and most ferocious challenges include money struggles, leadership burnout, and territorialism. Readers who have some experience with community initiatives will recognize these. And we believe that there is an important albeit complex connection between sustainability — riding out the storms — and strengths.

Building relationships, framing leadership, and constructing collective relevance are the strategies to raise the village. Anticipating the challenges that will rise up to oppose each of these, and knowing how to use strengths to overcome them, will arm early years collaboratives with the strength to sustain themselves.

RELATIONSHIP OBSTACLES: MONEY

*"The harder you fight to hold on
to specific assumptions, the more likely
there's gold in letting go of them."*
— JOHN SEELY BROWN, *FAST COMPANY*

Relationships have a greater chance of being sustained when a positive interaction occurs. People inherently want to be a part of something where they feel strong and valued and where they can contribute in a meaningful way.

This means people can be hooked into wanting to continue the relationship if leaders tap into peoples' strengths and orchestrate interactions to be successful and positive.

This is true for traditional and non-traditional partners. When able to use their strengths, they see that they have something unique and worthwhile to share and continue sharing. Strengths bring out the best in ourselves and in others, building community capacity and enabling collaboration in an ongoing way.

MONEY AS A BARRIER

Let's be honest: One of the biggest threats to sustained collaborative relationships is money. There's really no nice way to describe what typically happens to a group of people or organizations when dollars and cents are dangled before them. Even the most cohesive group can fall apart when money is introduced into the mix. It speaks, really, to the fragility of sustaining community relationships.

THE MONEY TRAIN

The whistle blows. The train is at the station. The train comes in infrequently, rarely long enough for passengers to determine where it's going or whether they really want to get on. But the train is here and it may not come again for a while. Who cares where it's going? Who cares what you might be leaving behind? Get on!

The passengers are panicking on the station platform, pushing and shoving and vying for seats. Conductors are suspiciously absent during the scramble.

The whistle blows again.

Those who have made it on sigh with relief. Those left behind sit anxiously with their belongings. They pull out remnants of a meal, partly finished crossword puzzles, and keep themselves occupied until the distant sound of another money train stirs their hope that this time they will manage to climb aboard.

More often than not, the direction and choices of communities are driven by money. The money train enters and leaves communities on no particular schedule and on no particular route.

Most social programs and services are funded in a patchwork way, stitched together from a variety of sources: government, charities, foundations, grants, local businesses, and consumers. Funding opportunities are usually created and distributed with narrow deliverables and strings attached. The end of the fiscal year brings short-term "pots of money" to be grabbed at by communities using the theme of the day.

The inconsistency of funding opportunities and allocation unavoidably creates the perception that funding is unpredictable and unfair. This perception feeds into the panic on the platform as the money train rolls in and out of town. The money train fragments services because it causes organizations to compete for dollars to fit the needs of the funding mandate instead of meeting the current needs of the people they serve.

What is the role of collaboratives in changing the story of the money train? How can strengths be better used to sustain collaborative relationships despite the inevitable struggle for program fiscal survival? We have demonstrated, through a focus on strengths, that relationships can be fortified not only to withstand the negative effects of funding competitions but also to slowly change the money train story to meet collaborative needs.

FROM CONCEPT TO REALITY

A small but vibrant non-profit organization offering literacy tutoring support to adults found itself well positioned for growth when literacy issues became a trendy political issue. The government of British Columbia had announced the bold goal of becoming the best-educated and most literate jurisdiction on the continent as it prepared to host the 2010 Winter Olympics.

Political promises, in the shadow of an election, usually bring money.

The literacy society was thrilled to find themselves the recipients of a government-matched fundraising opportunity bringing in thousands of dollars earmarked for literacy initiatives in that community. With the financial health of the literacy society secure, most of the incoming funds were available to be redirected and shared with other organizations that supported a broader population (from children to seniors) in the area of literacy.

The first year this funding was allocated, it was distributed like candy thrown to children at a parade: eagerly, randomly, and lacking in forethought. Basically the goal was just to get the candy to the most obvious or most convenient spectators. The second year demanded some forethought and a process that was transparent and felt fair. A more formal funding grant process was implemented based on the great information provided by the Work Group for Community Health and Development at the University of Kansas (ctb.ku.edu/en/).

The local early years collaborative offered to contribute their expertise to those who were thinking of applying for funds that would serve young children and their families. The collaborative did not want to screen, weed out, or pass judgment on any of the applications. It wanted to ensure that there was a forum for applicants to make collaborative connections before applying for the dollars. The idea behind this was to reduce duplication and enhance the capacity of each idea by building the relationships between involved organizations.

The concept was great and the reality was magic. The first open-door meeting was held on a weeknight. The meeting was well advertised because this opportunity had been promoted directly on the funding application. Nine organizations showed up, each with their own brewing ideas of projects and ways to use the potential grant dollars to serve young children. In a relaxed fashion, and with initially no discussion, each organization described their project ideas to the group.

Slowly but surely the room began to electrify as participants began to see the common thread weaving the initiatives together, strengthening them all. Once everything was out on the table, each group noted how well elements of other groups' ideas strengthened their own.

The proposal ideas were essentially the organizations' strengths wrapped around a literacy project concept. What transpired over the course of the evening was not only the connection of project ideas but also the complementing of strengths.

For example, one organization's proposal described the creation of a play-and-learn library for children. This agency had the strengths of space, lending items, and a vision of a well-organized, efficient lending system to families.

Another organization hoped to provide support to child-care providers through workshops on integrating play, literacy, and physical activity into their practice. Their strength was in educating service providers.

A third organization brought the strength of promoting play through concrete activities directly with children. Their approach used an evidence-based curriculum that required purchase and training. What they knew best was connecting directly with children.

The common thread was the strong emphasis on learning through play as a way to address literacy. It was exciting to see how each organization brought unique strengths that transformed a good concept into a fantastic full-spectrum approach.

Three organizations, later joined by two more, ended up putting in a joint application. The result? An even greater leveraging of existing resources than anticipated and the receipt of more monies overall than each organization had asked for on its own.

The exercise had a significant impact on relationships, too. Their interactions were better sustained because, as they pooled their strengths toward a common purpose, they found the best ways to work together on an ongoing basis. Their success with both the funding application and program delivery continues to inspire these organizations to be more aware of how to work together in a variety of situations. The significant effect at the community level was the demonstration that local organizations can influence how money is distributed when they decrease competition and increase collaboration.

HOW?

It is critical to anticipate the impact and influence that money can have on relationships. This can be done by thinking ahead and asking: Is there a process in place?

Such a process is more active than passive when it comes to funding: It involves being more assertive in applying for funds and development instead of merely accepting what is being handed out. This attitude can be developed and reinforced by stepping back as a group and determining how the group can contribute to the greater health of the community by being partners of and collaborators with other groups, acknowledging one another's strengths instead of scrambling for funds.

In support of early years community developers, following are some ideas to help collaboratives leverage the strengths of both individuals and groups to sustain the efforts of building relationships in the context of funding:

- Build in opportunities for people to share their innovative ideas about money and funding opportunities.
- Advocate with funding bodies that their applications ask for a demonstration of collaborative planning.
- Ask: If current funding stopped, would this group still be a sustainable collaborative? How can strengths be the investment to achieve group sustainability?
- Focus on leveraging partnerships, rather than just on fundraising.
- Recognize that the processes used at funder tables are most likely also used at community tables. Why not encourage merging the two? Bring key coordinators together from both funding and community tables.
- Acknowledge the strengths that funders can share with a collaborative (e.g., infrastructure, knowledge bases, and connections).

• Anticipate that working together (funders with community) may be messy and more time consuming but remain focused on the benefits of being more inclusive, more collaborative, and more "ground up."

LEADERSHIP: BURNOUT

"It is our collective task to liberate the leader
within each and every one of us."
— JAMES KOUZES AND BARRY POZNER, *A LEADER'S LEGACY*

The role of strengths to sustain leadership is fundamental to keeping a vibrant and innovative momentum in an early years collaborative. As this book continues to remind readers, there is no *one* way of doing the work. This is especially true when we consider how strengths can sustain leadership. When early years collaborative work is designed and structured on the unique strengths of participants, leadership will be fostered. When collaboratives are aware of strengths and call on them more often, people will be more likely to take on leadership roles.

Jennifer Fox (2008) writes in her book *Your Child's Strengths* that strengths work in ways that change lives and can become a thinking habit. Ideally, they will become not a skill to be learned but a way of thinking and ultimately a way of working together.

FIZZLE AND DIE

"It's always the same people." How many times have you heard this statement at a volunteer or community event or meeting? Maybe you've even heard it at an early years collaborative meeting. We have. The distress beneath the statement can sound an awful lot like a cry for help. When people complain that they need new blood to help out, they are likely verging on burnout. Burnout is an occupational hazard for people who are deeply committed and passionate and doing too many activities that drain them or leave them feeling unsatisfied.

How can leaders prevent, or at least reduce, the wearisome, energy-sucking effects of burnout? By helping others sustain themselves through strengths. Using strengths can stir up passion, interest, and excitement. Stress is reduced by focusing on strengths and sharing the load in activities that drain.

The notion that one man's junk is another man's treasure applies here. Maybe you consider some of the things you do to be junk, things that are a struggle for you or even things you do well but leave you feeling drained. These very things may be what someone else craves to be doing. Someone else may find what drains you to be a source of inspiration and energy.

This approach can also create opportunities for individuals to work alongside someone new. Break projects up into bits and pieces and intentionally seek the right "strength fit" for people to get the job done.

Staff turnover and burnout often go hand in hand. Take a situation in which a facilitator or a participant has worked with a collaborative, has invested time and energy into developing relationships and starting projects, and then leaves. The loss of this person can cause a major break in momentum.

The reasons for someone leaving are often unavoidable (retirement, relocation, education) or may be preventable (recognizing people's contributions, making them feel that they belong, giving them a break from work that drains them). Prevent or reduce negative feelings by drawing attention to strengths. Make time more often to use strengths in the work to increase satisfaction and to decrease feelings of isolation.

Facilitative leaders should consider using strengths thinking in their succession planning. There are many ways to approach succession planning. One of them is to embrace a team approach. Just imagine the richness of job sharing. This not only gives the organization access to completely different sets of skills, expertise, and strengths, but it also gives it the opportunity to divvy up tasks based on what best gives satisfaction. This way, when someone needs to move on, they don't take the entire driving core of the group with them.

We are speaking from experience here. We have spent time as cofacilitators and appreciate the dynamic blend of strengths that emerged. While this team approach may not be practical in many places, it is a creative way to consider filling the shoes of a position as complex as an early years community developer while freeing up each individual to play more to their strengths. Even if a formal team approach isn't feasible, consider the strengths of the whole collective. Give participants opportunities to play to their strengths in order to complement the strengths of a single facilitator.

HOW?

Knowing and using your strengths, both your own and the collaborative's, is a way to sustain leadership and prevent burnout. Strengths will energize you and remind you of your passion for the work. Here are ways strengths can be called upon:

- Create an opportunity to explore personal strengths.
- Notice what you enjoy doing and find out what gets other people fired up.
- Include strengths as part of an orientation procedure or package. Encourage new participants to discover and share their strengths right from the get-go.

- Connect people with differing strengths and skills on project subcommittees.
- Show your own vulnerabilities. This gives others permission to fill in the gaps.
- Acknowledge that people have strengths to offer that are unconnected to their job.
- Delegate: Don't try to be everything for every person — that may be robbing others of a chance to grow.

RELEVANCE: TERRITORY

"Life is like a band. We need not all play the same part, but we must all play in harmony."
— ANONYMOUS

L et's be real. Collective relevance isn't going to be present within groups at every given moment. However, as mentioned in chapter 13, it can be intentionally encouraged through dialogue — creating a space, phenomenological questions, creativity — *and* by focusing on strengths. How does a focus on strengths uphold the group magic, the seeing and feeling of the whole, or, in other words, the collective relevance?

Collective relevance can be generated by holding discussions about what makes individuals feel strong and then travelling beyond that to discover what makes them strong as a group. Think of the richness, the energy boost, and the validation to keep going that flows from a group exploration of what makes the group feel strong together. Answering this strength-filled question on an ongoing basis will bring the group's strengths into focus so that they can easily be accessed when things get tricky.

TERRITORY

Like all good things in life, including collective relevance, complexity is part and parcel of the process. Obstacles will be encountered. Some of the biggest ones to collective relevance will be territorial issues. Territorial or power struggles are as common to early years community development groups as crying is to a newborn baby.

Territorialism is a normal response when individuals who feel passionate about their individual organization's and/or personal mandates are expected to represent their interests in a collaborative setting or initiative. Finding the balance between being individual and collective at the same time can be challenging.

Territorialism will look and feel different for everyone. The following story reflects an example of how it can get in the way of collective relevance and how strengths can play a role in moving forward together.

FOR LEASE

The monthly agenda for an early years collaborative meeting included developing a mission statement. During this process, an impromptu discussion and brainstorming session was prompted by a question one of the participants asked: "What are the strengths of our network?" The ensuing conversation produced a list of strengths that spoke to connection and inclusion. One item was "building an honest and safe environment for sharing ideas and thoughts."

Sometime later, to the surprise of some of the collaborative members, one organization made a decision — as autonomous organizations are allowed and expected to do — that had potential implications for another organization.

Organization #1 was in need of additional programming space and became aware of an available building, located on the same property as Organization #2. Organization #1 made inquiries with the owner of the building — a third party in this case — to find if other agencies were interested in the space. The answer was no, so they proceeded to lease the building in question.

In fact, however, Organization #2 had hopes of using that same building space. Faced with the lost opportunity, Organization #2 felt sidelined by the third party and the other organization, with which they had worked in the local early years collaborative. You could have cut the tension with a knife. The sense of cohesion and trust within and between the organizations was damaged.

So why did this happen? Incorrect assumptions may very well have played a role. Or perhaps the third party was unaware that both organizations wanted the space. Confusion may have existed over what collaboration is and what level of collaboration each organization desired. An element of business competition may have been involved. A lack of communication was definitely a factor.

Regardless of the reasons behind the decisions in question, this experience unearthed some issues about individual operational decisions with implications for other local programming.

What was missing was the strength of the collaborative. If one of its strengths was to "build an honest and safe environment for sharing ideas and thoughts," then they failed. Organization #1 did not use the collaborative's strength to explore implications or consult more widely. Could they have taken the idea of individual expansion to the early years table while checking details for accuracy?

Although organizations have the right to operate autonomously, it is in everyone's best interest that they be transparent in program planning and whether potential conflict is anticipated. Organization #2 knew there was an impending vacancy. Could they have brought the opportunity to the collaborative at an early stage for group consideration? The relationship of the third party to the early years collaborative is still in question.

Each organization has strengths, services, and resources that complement one another. Who should or could convene a meeting to make it easier for organizations to put ideas and plans on the table? Could an early years collaborative with an objective facilitative leader ask key questions that could help to avoid territorial situations in the first place? These questions could include:

- Are there feelings of territorialism that need to be acknowledged?
- What are the collective implications of our actions?
- How do our strengths as an early years collaborative play into this?
- What are our goals in collaboration?

The result may or may not have been different had such questions been explored, but the resulting feelings of exclusion would not have occurred and strengths would have been at the forefront in any decision.

So, yes, territorialism is to be expected, but at times it can be avoided or dealt with by naming collective strengths and then ensuring that the strengths are actually used in community and organizational decisions.

HOW?

To avoid territorialism, provide opportunities for many voices to be heard. Consider some of the following approaches:

- *Memorandums of Understanding (MOU):* These are an example of how to formally address power or territory by agreeing to relevance: that is, what makes this work relevant to us collectively. This concept, often used at a regional level, can be adapted for smaller groups by creating team charters.

- *Early Learning Frameworks:* These are a way to bring people together by bridging systems and providing a common context for programs and projects that fall under a similar mandate. Make sure strengths come up.

• *Visual reminders:* Collective artwork, scrapbooks of accomplishments, calendars, and reflection cards are all ways to say: "We are a team, a collaborative, and we are strong."

• *"What's on the Horizon" discussions:* Share what's on the horizon at your next collaborative meeting. For example: Organization #1 can come to the table and share its individual mandate and current hopes and directions. Then the floor can be opened for discussion to see what organizations #2, #3, and #4 are doing, determine how they fit together, and formulate what they can create together.

• *Big thinker chart:* Go back to the collective relevance chapter and revisit the chart. Is it time to discuss, as a group, one or two of these concepts? For example: Revisit the collaboration continuum to address territorial issues when they happen or to discuss how people want to work together.

• *Collaborative list of strengths:* List and create your collaborative strengths as a group. Then actually *use* this list instead of just leaving it hidden in meeting minutes. Bring out the list during times of territorial or other conflict and ask how the situation at hand can be helped with the collective strengths.

• *Allow conflict to emerge:* Get the elephants out from under the table. Sometimes people have to vent, talk about hard issues, and generally beat topics to death. Watch for the richness and growth in this process and the readiness to move on constructively with the work. Acknowledge common issues, concerns, and feelings of being threatened. Help participants feel that the collaborative work is relevant and meaningful and that it is grounded in making a difference.

And don't forget to celebrate your strengths.

CELEBRATING

Celebrations confirm a sense of belonging. A birthday party says: You made it this far — congratulations! In a birthday party, you are surrounded by friends and family. Your place in the world is confirmed, honoured, and shaped by others. Celebrating in an early years development context shares a few of these qualities. It is a chance to say: Look what we have done so far. It also connects those who have contributed with one another, validating a sense of interconnectedness and collective strength.

Nurturing that sense of belonging is like the icing on the cake. It propels participants as a group toward collective relevance.

What does a celebration look like? It certainly doesn't have to include balloons and cake, although that is sometimes fun. Check out this list for ideas:

- Take the time to get to know one another on a personal level.
- Take the time to reflect over the year and share and record accomplishments from different perspectives.
- Honour how the collaborative grows and learns from any mistakes along the way.
- Share special food together.
- Allow participants to share what they are proudest of in their involvement with the early years collaborative.
- Make time during meetings for organizations to show and tell.
- Host special events that feed the passion of the collaborative, such as professional development and personal development opportunities.

Something to think about: How do you balance celebrating individuals, organizations, and the collaborative? At what point does honouring individuals fuel a competitive spirit over a team spirit? What are the implications of public recognition on the collaborative? The point of celebration is to enhance connections and harness the momentum of the group. Brian Stanfield writes that, "Honoring the group requires the ability to recognize the wonder of life and the essential greatness of each human being" (Stanfield, 2002, p. 114).

STRENGTHS TO SUSTAIN

There is little point in inspiring, creating, and beginning to build a village without the commitment — and a plan — to sustain the effort. Good intentions go only so far. One-hit wonders are just that, and pilot projects on top of pilot projects don't serve anyone well. Early years community development works best when it is ongoing — with no defined end destination. The cycle includes: visioning, learning, planning, action, and evaluation.

In 2008 Barack Obama won a substantial victory in the US federal election using a simple message, "Yes, we can." Citizens of the United States, and literally around the globe, were thirsty for the hope and confidence that a positive, strength-based direction could lead. In like manner, in the work of early years collaboratives the message, the hook, and the glitz must hold more than a promise or hint of reaching a desired and alternative future. It must be coupled with the intentional activities that are grounded in strengths. If it is just the glitzy political messages on the surface with no intentional activity, all will be meaningless.

Supporting children in their first few years, as it happens, supports future parents, their children, and their grandchildren as well — if the collaborative efforts are sustained and the village takes on the responsibility of raising its children, that is. In the world of one-time funding and flash-in-the-pan success stories, how can village-raising be sustained? We believe the answer is by intentionally applying strengths.

"I THINK WE CAN DO IT AGAIN"

The children continue playing. After the new materials from Grace's structure are transplanted to the common area, we hear from Tanner, the boy with a plan.

Taking on the job of foreman he gives an order: "We need to make a wall now. This block goes there."

The new concept is easily accepted by the girls. Morgan voices a fact: "We need more blocks."

All four children are now building with every available block, their excitement fuelled by the quickly growing castle. Musical chatter is followed by moments of quiet work and thoughtful placement of materials. After some time of creative play, the structure tumbles yet again.

Grace takes on the role of assistant and passes Tanner one of the fallen blocks. Tanner, his focus elsewhere, disregards the offer and says, "I don't need that one."

The educator wonders how Grace feels about having her offer of help rejected. She comments approvingly, "That was friendly, Grace."

Tanner hears this and turns from the blocks to Grace. He says, "I don't need . . ." but then changes his mind and says, "Grace, now I need that."

Grace passes more blocks to Tanner, pleased to be involved.

Brynn tries to crawl into the castle, and guess what? Yes, the blocks plummet to the ground yet again.

The educator sees this as an opportunity and calls out, "Shall we make it bigger?"

Morgan responds with gusto, "I think we can do it again!"

This may be enough of the observation to illustrate sustainability, but wait . . . there's more. The children's play is expanded in many ways. They use the blocks as a balance beam, as a way to play hide and seek by burying each other, and also as a roadway for the vehicles the educator had brought in her magic bag and handed out to extend the play.

Eventually the children lose interest in the blocks and are ready to move on to something else.

The educator keeps the momentum going. She asks the group, "Who can help me hold the bag and clean up all these blocks?"

The challenge works; the builders become cleaners. They work together to return the village materials into the depths of the bag, but the village connections remain.

The educator hints that there will be a celebration afterward to honour their teamwork. She leads the captivated foursome to the trunk of her car where the surprise awaits. The trunk opens to reveal a treasure-trove of books: each child receives a special gift to remind them of their day.

It's getting late. But because their young bodies are fuelled with activity and excitement, they continue to skip, run, and play.

The educator follows their lead as they venture to the backyard, poised and ready for something new. There are new discoveries to explore, new things to be built, new ties and connections to be strengthened.

And with the words "We can do it again!" reverberating in their heads, there are more villages to be raised.

ACTIVITY #13

STRENGTHS DISCOVERY

General Idea

Use questions to discover personal strengths. Explore what makes each individual of the collaborative strong.

STEP 1

Self-reflection: Take a moment to think about your strengths. Strengths can be hard to describe, so think of a task you love to do or an activity or a time that left you feeling fulfilled.

STEP 2

In pairs, take turns describing your thought, or give an example of a time when you felt strong.

STEP 3

Ask questions of one another. Help each other explore personal strengths. This is the time to get specific about strengths, to give what is hard to describe some very describable details! Try some of the following questions with a partner.

> Fill in these statements and share your answers with a partner:
>
> I'm at my best when...
>
> I feel strong when...
>
> I can't wait to...
>
> Time flies by when...

> Reach an even deeper understanding together. Ask your partner to describe:
>
> What is it about *(answer from above)* you love?
>
> What is it about *(answer from above)* that makes you feel strong?
>
> When do you like to do this *(answer from above)*?

STEP 4

After exploring the questions, claim the strength!

• *Variation:* Ask more self-reflective questions: How can you create more opportunities to use this strength and how will being aware of your strength assist you in the collaborative personally? How will you discover more about your other strengths or reach a place of deeper understanding?

• *Variation:* Move from an individual focus on strengths to a community focus. Draw puzzle shapes on paper, cut them out, and give one to each person. Ask them to write a specific strength on this puzzle piece.

Have the individuals form a circle and, one by one, read out their strength. As they do so, they join their puzzle piece to the others on the floor until all the pieces are connected. This shows how a community is full of individual strengths and how the strengths have potential to unite the group.

ACTIVITY #14

ANTICIPATING HICCUPS AND BUMPS

General Idea

The reality is that collaborative groups will encounter challenges. When these challenges are anticipated, the chance of devastating impacts is lessened. Use this group activity to be forward thinking, to increase group resilience, and to explore barriers from multiple perspectives.

What's Worked for Us . . .

STEP 1

As a group, identify one possible (or pending) challenge to the group. For example, in one session we targeted a situation in which local non-profit organizations were so busy searching for funding to survive that they were unable to participate in collaborative activities and were feeling competitive about local funding opportunities.

STEP 2

Using a handout consisting of twelve empty squares, ask each participant to write in three strengths — one in each square — that the collaborative has that may help overcome the identified hiccup.

STEP 3

Ask participants to get up and mingle. With each person they meet, have them offer *one* strategy from their list and receive *one* strategy from the other. They write these in the blank squares. Exchange no more than one strategy with any given partner.

STEP 4

Repeat the process until all the squares are full. Note: If the two lists are identical, the pair must brainstorm and create a new idea.

STEP 5

In the large group, create and discuss a master list of the collaborative's strengths. Apply these strengths toward action to support the current hiccup, or keep them in reserve until you hit a bump.

ACTIVITY #15

THANK YOU, THANK YOU, THANK YOU

General Idea

Thank-yous help to build bridges, sustain relationships, and celebrate accomplishments. This activity engages people to get involved in thanking partners in a fun and meaningful way.

What's Worked for Us . . .

STEP 1

As a large group, brainstorm a list of everyone who may be considered a partner. This list should include people and organizations that contribute in many different ways to local early years efforts.

STEP 2

Provide the group with a selection of craft supplies: cards, envelopes, stickers, glue sticks, fancy paper, and wording. We printed white paper with expressions such as: "Thank you" and "You are a valued partner." Crafters will help non-crafters. Allow the session to become an informal networking opportunity as you create custom thank-you cards.

STEP 3

Someone will need to take charge of the list and collect mailing addresses for each identified partner. Drop them off or mail them at a later date. Feel good that the cards reflect a collective appreciation.

CONCLUSION

A lexis Carrel writes that "the first duty of society is to give each of its members the possibility of fulfilling his destiny. When it becomes incapable of performing this duty it must be transformed" (Carrel, 1952, p. 145). The implications for communities that create the villages we are advocating for are massive — and so are the implications of doing nothing.

Let's create an expectation that children will grow up surrounded by family, friends, and even strangers who care for them and love them.

Let's keep childish energy and wonder alive in the hearts of adults and in the workings of institutions.

Let's validate the critical role that families play in the village by reflecting their importance in local and global decisions.

Let's bring a natural compassion into the social and business systems by keeping children a priority.

As a society, let's take bold steps to tackle complex social issues with confidence and conviction.

It takes a village to raise a child, but are we ready to raise the village?

THE EVIDENCE IS CLEAR

Research demonstrates that to make the greatest difference in the trajectory of a person's life, positive experiences in a nurturing environment must exist during that person's early years. Biology, neurobiology, sociology, and epidemiology promote early support to families with young children.

THE PARTNERS EXIST

More and more organizations, when faced with complex community problems, are seeing the value of prevention. The world of early years has broadened beyond early childhood education and child care. Education, health, social services, business, faith-based communities, urban planning, human resources, and academic research have recognized that some of the solutions to the problems we face today need to be implemented early and often for tomorrow's youth, tomorrow's employees, and tomorrow's seniors.

THE POLITICAL STAGE IS SET

It is significant to have the United Nations, UNICEF, the Organization for Cooperation and Economic Development, and the World Health Organization as backups. Their benchmarks, standards, and international recommendations leverage the needed awareness at all levels of government. Early child development is not republican, nor is it democratic, conservative, liberal, or green. There is a place for any and all of the existing political bents to get a strong foothold on policies that support children and assist in elevating the profile of early years collaborative work.

THE TOOLS ARE KNOWN

This book contains many ideas tailored specifically to early years community development. These ideas are not brand new; they were born from the grassroots efforts of people around the world, from community development practices, and from the cultural teachings that guide our societies. They are gentle guides to help people figure out how to create positive change together. Behind the use of any idea is the quintessence of our virtues, behaviours, attitudes, and choices.

THE TIME TO TALK IS NOW

In the time it takes to count to five, eight babies are born around the world. With each child comes the opportunity to make a difference, the opportunity to add to the vibrancy of our villages. With evidence, partners, politics, and tools at your disposal, the village needs *you* to find your relevance and to continue offering your strengths through relationships and leadership. So the answer to the question is — yes, we are ready to raise the village!

REFERENCES

Alberni Valley Make Children First Network. (2009). Parent voice brochure. (Online). http://www.albernichildrenfirst.ca/modules/resources/index.php?id=3

Allender, Dan B. (2006). *Leading with a limp: Turning your struggles into strengths.* Colorado Springs: WaterBrook Press.

B.C. Council for the Family. (2007). B.C. experience of parenting poll. (Online). http://bccf.bc.ca/hm/inside.php?id=45

BC Healthy Communities. (2006). Integral community capacity building framework. (Online). http://www.bchealthycommunities.ca/Content/Our%20 Approach/Integral%20Approaches%20to%20Community%20 Capacity.asp

Barber, Anne & Waymon, Lynn. (1992). *Great connections: Small talk and networking for business people.* Manassas: Impact! Publications.

Barth, Roland. (1991). *Improving schools from within: Teachers, parents and principals can make the difference.* New York: Wiley.

Block, Peter. (2008). *Community: The structure of belonging.* San Francisco: Berrett-Koehler.

Bohm, David, Factor, Don & Garrett, Peter. (1991). Dialogue: A proposal. (Online.) http://www.infed.org/archives/e-texts/bohm_dialogue.htm

Buckingham, Marcus. (2006). *Trombone player wanted.* DVD. Marcus Buckingham Company.

Buckingham, Marcus. (2008). *The truth about you: Your secret to success.* Nashville: Thomas Nelson.

Carrel, Alexis. (1952). *Reflections on life.* New York: Hawthorn Books.

Chrislip, David D. (2002). *The collaborative leadership fieldbook.* San Francisco: Jossey-Bass.

Clifton, Donald & Nelson, Paul. (1995). *Soar with your strengths.* New York: Dell.

Cohen, Larry, Chavez, Vivian & Chehimi, Sana. (2007). *Prevention is primary: Strategies for community well-being.* San Francisco: Jossey-Bass.

Corbett, D. (2002). *Understanding the context for collaboration.* Master's thesis, Royal Roads University.

Corning, Peter. (1983). *The synergism hypothesis: A theory of progressive evolution.* New York: McGraw-Hill.

Covey, Stephen R. (2004). *The seven habits of highly effective people.* New York: Simon & Schuster.

Damon, William. (2006). Finding noble purpose. From the program for the Vancouver Dialogues, Dalai Lama Center for Peace and Education.

Dreher, Diane. (1996). *The tao of personal leadership*. New York: Collins Business.

Durkheim, Emile & Swain, Joseph Ward. (1976). *The elementary forms of the religious life*. (2nd ed.). New York: HarperCollins.

Early childhood development evaluation. (2009). (Online). http://www.successby6bc.ca/early-childhood-development

Early Years Community Development Conference. (2008, March). Harrison Hot Springs, B.C.

Eiseley, Loren. (1979). *The star thrower*. Fort Washington: Harvest Books.

Fox, Jennifer. (2008). *Your child's strengths: Discover them, develop them, use them*. New York: Viking.

Gladwell, Malcolm. 2002. *The tipping point: How little things can make a big difference*. Boston: Back Bay Books.

Goldman, H. & Intriligator, B.A. (1990). Factors that enhance collaboration among education, health and social service agencies. Paper presented at the Annual Meeting of the American Educational Research Association. Boston. (Online). http://www.eric.ed.gov/ERICDocs/data/ericdocs2sql/content_ storage_01/0000019b/80/20/33/30.pdf

Goleman, Daniel. (2006). *Social intelligence: The new science of human relationships*. New York: Bantam.

Gonzalez-Mena, Janet. (2009). *Child, family, and community: Family-centered early care and education*. (5th ed.). Upper Saddle River: Pearson Education.

Grant, Ali & Steele, Margaret. (2009). Getting to the root of it: A dialogue on affecting quality of life in the Alberni Valley. Consultation conducted by AMG Consulting, Vancouver.

Gray, Barbara. (1989). *Collaborating: Finding common ground for multiparty problems*. San Francisco: Jossey-Bass.

Hertzman, Clyde & Irwin, Lori. (2007). It takes a child to raise a community: Population-based measurement of early child development. (Online). http://www.earlylearning.ubc.ca/documents/2007/It%20Takes%20a%20Child%20HELP%20Brief%20July%202007.pdf (Human Early Learning Partnership).

Hunter, Dale, Bailey, Anne & Taylor, Bill. (1995). *The art of facilitation: How to create group synergy.* Cambridge, MA: Da Capo Press.

Irwin, Lori, Siddiqi, Arjumand & Hertzman, Clyde. (2007). Early child development: A powerful equalizer. Final report, World Health Organization's Commission on Social Determinants of Health.

Isaacs, William. (1999). *Dialogue: The art of thinking together.* New York: Broadway Business.

Joyce, Stephen James. (2007). *Teaching an anthill to fetch: Developing collaborative intelligence @ work.* Alberta: Mighty Small Books Publishing.

Kershaw, Paul. (2009). About SC2 Research Network. (Online). http://www.earlylearning.ubc.ca/sc2/index.html (Human Early Learning Partnership).

Kordesh, Richard. (2006). *Restoring power to parents and places: The case for family-based community development.* Lincoln: iUniverse.

Kouzes, James M. & Pozner, Barry Z. (2002). *The leadership challenge.* (3rd ed.). New York: Jossey-Bass.

Lennard, Henry & Crowhurst-Lennard, Suzanne. (2000). *The forgotten child.* Carmel: Gondolier Press.

Make Children First Kamloops. (retrieved 2009). Growing up in Kamloops parent survey. (Online). http://www.makechildrenfirst.ca/cms/index.php/committees/growing-up-in-kamloops/growing-up-in-kamloops-parent-survey.html

Matthews, Hannah & Ewen, Danielle. (2006). *Reaching all children? Understanding early care and education participation among immigrant families.* (Online). http://www.clasp.org/ publications/child_care_immigrant.pdf (Center for Law and Social Policy).

Mbogoni, Lawrence. (1996). H-Africa. (Online). http://www.h-net. org/~africa/threads/village.html

McCain, Margaret Norrie, Mustard, J. Fraser & Shanker, Stuart. (2007). *Early years study 2: Putting science into action.* Toronto: Council for Early Child Development.

McLeod, Donna & Russell, Varina. (2007). *Course CVIH 920, Module 6: Community collaborations in support of child and youth.* Toronto: Ryerson University.

Mintzberg, Henry. (2004). *Managers not MBA's: A hard look at the soft practice of managing and management development.* San Francisco: Berrett-Koehler.

Motwane, Aman A. (2000). *The power of wisdom: When you change how you see the world, your whole world changes.* Hermona Beach: Prakash Press.

Orey, Michael (Ed.). (2004). Emerging perspectives on learning, teaching and technology. (Online). http://projects.coe.uga.edu/ epltt/ (University of Georgia).

Owen, Harrison. (1997). *Open space technology: A user's guide.* San Francisco: Berrett-Koehler.

Pascal, Blaise. (2007). *Blaise Pascal: Thoughts, letters, and minor works.* New York: Cosimo Classics.

Perkins, David. (2003). *King Arthur's round table: How collaborative conversations create smart organizations.* Hoboken: Wiley.

Putnam, Robert D. (2000). *Bowling alone: The collapse and revival of American community.* New York: Simon & Schuster.

Rampanen, John. (2007). *Nananiiqsuu haahuupa* presentation hosted by Alberni Valley Make Children First Network, Port Alberni, B.C.

Rinaldi, Carlina. (2005). *In dialogue with Reggio Emilia: Listening, researching, and learning.* Reggio Emilia, Italy: Reggio Children Publications.

Sawyer, Keith. (2007). *Group genius: The creative power of collaboration.* New York: Basic Books.

Schroeder, Joanne. (2006, February). Building a provincial community development network for young children, Early Years Conference: Child Development Practices: A Decade of Change, Vancouver, B.C. Interprofessional Continuing Education, University of British Columbia.

Senge, Peter, Scharmer, C. Otto, Jaworski, Joseph & Flowers, Betty Sue. (2005). *Presence: An exploration of profound change in people, organizations, and society.* New York: Broadway Business.

Stanfield, R. Brian. (2002). *The workshop book: From individual creativity to group action.* Gabriola Island: New Society.

Sutherland, Anne & Thompson, Beth. (2001). *Kidfluence: Why kids today mean business.* New York: McGraw-Hill.

Torjman, Sherri. (2006). *Shared space: The communities agenda.* (Online). http://www.caledoninst.org/Publications/ PDF/603ENG.pdf

Vogt, Eric, Brown, Juanita & Isaacs, David. (2003). *The art of powerful questions: Catalyzing insight, innovation, and action.* Norfolk: Whole System Associates.

Westley, Frances, Zimmerman, Brenda & Patton, Michael. (2006). *Getting to maybe: How the world is changed.* Toronto: Random House Canada.

Wheatley, Margaret. (1992). *Leadership and the new science.* San Francisco: Berrett-Koehler.

Wheatley, Margaret. (1999). Servant leadership and community leadership in the 21st century. Keynote address. (Online). http://www.margaretwheatley.com/articles/servantleader.html

Wheatley, Margaret & Frieze, Deborah. (2006). Using emergence to take social innovations to scale. (Online). http://www.margaretwheatley.com/articles/emergence.html

Work Group for Community Health and Development at the University of Kansas. (2009). The community toolbox. (Online). http://ctb.ku.edu/en/

Yankelovich, Daniel. (1999). *The magic of dialogue: Transforming conflict into cooperation.* New York: Touchstone.

INDEX

ABOUT THE AUTHORS

TRACY SMYTH (left) has spent fifteen years helping individuals and communities articulate and achieve their goals for better social health. In 2001, with experience in public health, she became the community facilitator and implementation manager of a cutting-edge provincial program called Make Children First. In this role, she subsequently led one of three British Columbia communities into the world of early years community development. The successful initiative has generated a province-wide network of communities beginning their own community development journeys. In 2006 Tracy completed a master of arts degree in leadership and training at Royal Roads University. Her thesis examines multi-agency collaboration among senior management in large public institutions.

TAMMY DEWAR holds over twenty years of frontline experience as an early childhood educator and social service worker. Through her education and professional experience, Tammy has developed expertise in facilitating teams using collective, creative, and inclusive processes. After many years working with child, youth, and parent programs, Tammy joined the early years movement in 2006, bringing a fresh and inventive approach to promoting early childhood awareness and community planning. In addition, Tammy completed Ryerson University's first Community Collaborations in Support of Children and Youth interdisciplinary course.

Tracy and Tammy of Raising the Village Consulting provide learning experiences to engage individuals, organizations and communities in their efforts to collaborate with a focus on children.

For more information on Raising the Village
go to the Website

www.raisingthevillage.ca